Crossing Sydney

By

Susan L. Pare'

CROSSING SYDNEY: All contents copyright © 2015 Susan L. Pare'. All rights reserved. Printed in the United States of America.
ISBN13: 978-0-9966195-0-9

www.susanlpare.com

<u>Dedication</u>

To Wendy – Thank you for your help in proofing this book. She gave me the confidence to go one step further and share my words with my readers.

To Suzie, for her help and encouragement. She is special in so many ways.

To Herb. I'm sorry I beat you up when I was twelve.

Contents

CROSSING SYDNEY

BY

Susan L. Paré

One

The first time I killed someone it was an accident. I was angry but not so angry that I didn't know what I was doing. I wasn't in an uncontrollable rage. My only excuse is that I was pissed off because he wouldn't give me back my baseball.

So, at the age of twelve, when I picked up that baseball bat and hit Herb in the back of the head, I knew exactly what I was doing. I just didn't know he would die.

I only hit him once, but it was a mighty swing and he went down and stayed down. It seemed that there was an awful lot of blood gushing out of the back of his head. The sight of blood had never bothered me before but the amount pooling under his head made me just a little queasy.

The sound of my name being called blew through the wind and reached my ears. It was time to leave the little park and get home. I looked around but saw no one watching. I glanced down at Herb. He had not moved. I had never seen a dead body but I was pretty sure I was looking at my first.

My heart started pounding with excitement. I wanted to touch him. I wanted to know what a dead person felt like. As I started to bend down to touch his face, I heard my mother calling me once more. I turned away from him and ran the short block to my house where everyone was piling into the car. We were heading out on vacation.

"I just need to use the washroom before we leave," I

yelled at my mother and ran into the house. I was still holding the bat so I headed down to the basement to put it back in its proper place. Then I noticed a little patch of brown hair mixed with blood on the end of the bat. The laundry sink was right there in the same room, so I turned on the faucet and did a quick wash of the bat, making sure there was no blood or hair left in the sink.

As soon as I put the bat away, I was up the stairs, out the door, and in the car ready to leave for our summer trip out west. We were three miles out of town before I remembered that I had left my baseball in the park. It was still lying on the ground next to Herb. I figured I was fucked.

Our family spent the next two and a half months vacationing in Montana. By the time we arrived, back home the talk about Herb's death was old news. Of course, our family was shocked that such a thing could have happened so close to our home.

We were told that a vagrant had found Herb late in the afternoon, the same day that he was killed. The vagrant was questioned and finally released, as there was no solid evidence against him. The murder weapon was never found and Herb's death was never solved.

After I found out that Herb had died, I wondered if I would have been caught if we hadn't been leaving to go on vacation a few minutes after I hit him. The timing was beautiful and no one even knew we were still in town when the killing took place. No one investigating the murder even considered that the baseball might be a clue. They just figured it was Herb's baseball, so there was no follow-up and this information was discarded.

I knew I had lucked out. I also realized that I had better start to control that feeling that came over me when someone pissed me off. I just might not be so lucky the next time.

Two

I'm sitting in the Federal Building in downtown Chicago talking to Special Agent Bill Weatherby, who may be an agent but acts more like a secretary. I explain to him that I need to talk to the person in charge and no one else. He tells me that I need an appointment and to come back. "Forget it," I say and stand up. "I made a mistake coming here and I'm not making an appointment and I'm definitely not coming back."

"What could possibly be so important that you have to see him right this minute? What's this about anyway?" Special Agent Weatherby asks in a sarcastic tone.

"I'm dying, So Very Special Agent Weatherby," I sarcastically reply. "I've got information about several unsolved murders. I thought I should set the record straight before I'm dead. However, if your boss is just too busy to be bothered then forget about it."

He sighs and says, "Hold on. Just take a chair. I'll be right back."

I decide to sit back down. In less than two minutes, he's back and says, "Senior Special Agent Carroll will see you now."

I give him a look. It has taken me weeks to decide to make this move and now I'm getting the runaround. Perhaps it would be better to just get the hell out of here now. I've reached the point where I don't know what I'm doing anymore and coming here was definitely a mistake.

"Well, I don't want to see him. I told you that I wanted to talk to the Special Agent-in-Charge. Fuck it. I'm out of here," I tell him.

With that, I get up and walk out. He calls after me but I ignore him and head to the elevators. Just as I reach the elevators, the doors open and I walk right in and push the down button. Special Agent Weatherby is coming down the hall, yelling at me to stop, but he's too late and the doors shut.

I take the trip down to the main floor and head to the outside doors. I need a drink, but I quit drinking years ago. To hell with it. I'm finding a bar and I'm going to get good and drunk. Decision made and I already know that I won't do it.

I go through the revolving doors and stand on the sidewalk waiting for a cab to appear so I can flag it down. I need to get to Union Station and get my ass back home.

It's a little over an hour train ride and during this time I think about what I have just done. Walking into the Federal Building and telling someone that I had information about murders may not have been the good idea I thought it was. Why in God's name was I getting a conscience now? All the horrible things I've done in my life that never bothered me and now that I'm dying, I need to clear my conscience?

Stupid, stupid.

Maybe I just need to tell someone. I've kept all this to myself all these years. Perhaps I should just go find a priest. Will a priest listen to a confession if you're not Catholic? He can't tell anyone what you tell him, can he?

Am I looking for forgiveness? Of course not. There is no way I can be forgiven for all the things I've done. Besides, I'm not sorry. Not really.

It's the cancer. I haven't been thinking straight for a while now. You think you've kicked cancer in the butt and it comes back and bites you in the ass. Or, in my case, the brain. At the most, I have six months to live and a lot less than that before my decision-making is totally messed up.

The train pulls into the station and I debark, walk to my car, and drive home. I'll decide what to do tomorrow.

Three

I wake up this next morning refreshed and without a headache. That's new. Usually, it takes a few hours after taking my medicine before the headaches go away. Perhaps it's because I've made a decision and decided to see a psychiatrist. Supposedly, everything you tell a psychiatrist is confidential and, if that's true, I can finally tell my story.

I have a cup of coffee and start checking different doctors' credentials on the internet. I decided to see a Dr. Gabriel Miller, who has an office in Munster near the hospital. He has a five-star rating from his patients and has been in practice for seventeen years. Figuring he will do; I call to make an appointment. Jennie, the receptionist tells me that Dr. Miller is not taking new patients.

"I have cancer and I'm dying and I really need someone to talk to, Jennie. Is there any possibility that Dr. Miller could fit me in for a couple of visits for the next few weeks?" I ask.

After a brief moment of silence, Jennie asks me for a phone number and says she will get back to me. I end the call after giving her the information she needs to call me back.

Not even five minutes pass before my cell rings. I answer it and it is Jennie. She tells me that there is an opening on Dr. Miller's calendar for the next day at 2:00 pm if I am still interested. I take it.

The first part of my meeting with Dr. Miller is awkward. He is very soft-spoken and I have to listen extremely hard to hear everything he is saying. I finally ask him if he could speak up, as my disease has affected my hearing. He apologizes and says he will speak louder.

"I've never done this before and I don't know where to start," I tell him.

"Why don't you just tell me why you are here? My receptionist told me that you are dying. I'm sorry to hear that. If talking to me will help you get through this then by all means let me help you," Dr. Miller tells me.

"Doctor, before I tell you anything I need to know that everything I say to you will be confidential. I have a lot to get off my chest—a lot of bad things. I need to know that as long as I'm still living our conversations will not be repeated."

"You are protected by patient-doctor confidentiality. Nothing you tell me will be repeated. The law does, however, require me to inform them if something you tell me means that someone is in danger and a crime is going to be committed," Dr. Miller said.

"What about past crimes?" I ask.

"If you have committed previous crimes, I am not obligated to tell anyone and everything you tell me will be confidential," he replies.

"I'd like to start at the beginning and I'd like you to tape our sessions or whatever it is you do. I will probably be dead in six months. Possibly sooner. Once I die, I would like you to take the information I am about to share with you and turn it over to the FBI."

"The FBI?" he asks.

"There are some open cases that need to be closed and families that should be notified. I'm not sorry for what I have done but, for reasons I cannot explain, it has suddenly become important to me that people know the truth. Perhaps it's the cancer pushing on my brain but, whatever the reason, I need to do this."

"Well, then let's get started. I need some information before we get into it. Our records are incomplete so I'm going to ask you to fill in the blanks. I need your address, next of kin, and contact information. I would like a complete medical history and I need to know what drugs you are taking. Who is your oncologist? "

"My oncologist is Dr. Ann Fuller. As far as all that other stuff—well, you don't need that information to listen to me. Let's just say that I am alone. I have no family and there is no one to contact."

"I'm sorry, Sydney, but I need to have complete records as there are certain guidelines that I have to go by. We don't need the completed forms today but I would like you to take them home with you and fill them out. You can bring them with you when you come for your next visit."

"Fine, just give them to me and I'll fill them out," I

reply

"I'm extremely interested in what you have to say and I'd like to try to help you. How about we set up a couple of appointments for next week? I've checked with Jennie and she says we have some open time on Wednesday and Friday. Can you come in at 4:00 pm? I need to do some shuffling around of other patients, but I think it's doable. How does that sound to you?"

"I don't think two appointments will even begin to cover it," I reply.

"Seriously?"

"Doctor, I've been killing for years. I doubt very much I can tell you everything in a couple of hours."

"Excuse me a minute, Sydney," he says as he gets up and leaves the room.

A few minutes later Dr. Miller is back in his chair and tells me, "I'm switching some patients around to make time for you. How about coming in every day at four o'clock for the next couple of weeks?"

"That's great. I'm anxious to get started and I need to do this before I change my mind. So, that's it for today? We start tomorrow at four then?" I answered.

"Tomorrow," he replied.

I thank him and leave.

Four

My first session with Dr. Miller started at exactly four o'clock. I like his office and the way he has decorated it. Beside his desk, which is uncluttered, there are two large bookcases, a couple of chairs, a small table, and a couch. The walls of the room display his framed degrees and a couple of oil paintings.

We sit in the chairs facing each other. The small table separates us. The table holds a box of Kleenex and a large round ashtray. "You allow smoking?" I ask.

"No. Even though I have a wastebasket within reach, most people were tossing their used Kleenex on the table. Now they aim for the ashtray and it makes clean-up a little easier. Do you smoke?"

"Did years ago, but quit. Perhaps I should start up again. Nothing to lose now, right?"

"Are you comfortable?" Dr. Miller asks, ignoring my question.

"Very. This is a comfortable chair."

"You have a choice of the chair or the couch. Whatever you are comfortable with."

"I'll probably give the couch a try one of these visits," I say.

"After you left yesterday, I thought about our visit for a long time. I was trying to decide the best way to address your situation, as I get the feeling you have quite a lot to get off your chest. You mentioned you have done bad things. I think you should just tell me in your own words what you want to say. If there is something I need to address, I'll interrupt you. Mostly though, Sydney, I'm just going to listen while I record our sessions. Are you ready to start?"

"I think so. I've thought about our sessions, also, and how to address them. I've never told any of this to anyone and it's going to be hard. I guess it's best to just start at the beginning and work forward," I say. "Before I do that, however, let me tell you about some news that I recently got from my oncologist, which could explain a lot. A few months ago, I had an MRI of my brain. Of course, the cancer showed up, but so did something else. It also showed signs of moderate traumatic brain injury, which probably happened when I was young. I had two serious concussions. The first time my sister was pushing me on a swing. I fell off and hit my head on a rock, and was knocked unconscious. The second time I was hit in the head with a baseball bat, which is kind of funny when you think about it. Sorry. For years I've had..."

"Excuse me, but why do you find that funny?" Dr. Miller interrupted.

"Well, that's the way I murdered Herb," I replied.

"And, you're going to tell me about Herb?"

"Of course. Anyway, for years I suffered from horrible headaches. I would wake up screaming my head hurt so much. My parents did nothing but give me an aspirin and tell me to go back to bed. Over the years, the headaches lessened in severity, but they never quite went away. I don't know if this is an underlying cause but perhaps it explains why I have done some of the things I've done."

"Would you care to talk about your parents during our sessions?" Dr. Miller asked.

"Not really, I don't know if they are relevant at this point. I think I should start by telling you about Herb. Makes sense to start at the first one."

"Your first murder?" asks Dr. Miller.

"That's right," I reply.

"I was twelve years old and we were leaving town for the summer to vacation in Montana." I start.

I finish telling him the story.

"How do you feel?" the doctor asked me.

"It felt good to tell you. I never realized until recently how important it is for me to talk about this. I imagine it's the cancer. My brain gets confused lately and I find myself doing dumb things. A few weeks ago, I wouldn't have imagined that I would ever tell anyone about this. Is our time up?"

"Just about but I want to know how you felt after you killed Herb. What did you think about what you had done and how did you feel? You were only twelve years old and you had just killed someone. Were you remorseful?"

"First of all, I wasn't positive that he was dead or dying when I left him there. I would like nothing better than to tell you I felt sorry or sad when I found out he was dead. I'd like to say that I regretted what I had done. But, I didn't. Even to this day, when I get pissed off, I need to get even. At the age of twelve, I didn't control that emotion or even try. Now I do. I've learned to be patient and how to plan. I haven't been caught after all these years. You want to know how I felt after I hit Herb? Good. I really felt good. But when I found out I had killed him I got a thrill. Maybe satisfied would describe it. Yes, I think that satisfied would describe how I felt after I killed Herb."

"You felt no remorse at all?" Dr. Miller asked.

"I've never felt remorse over anything I've ever done," I replied.

"I see. Well, then, I'll see you tomorrow, Sydney."

"Bye, Doctor."

<u>Five</u>

By the time I entered high school, I had pretty much learned how to control my temper. It wasn't easy and believe me, there were a few times that I wanted to lash out and kill some idiot. Sometimes all it took was for some kid to bump into me in the hallway for me to start to lose it, but I learned control. I think fear was the biggest factor that kept me from following through, right then and there. I'd come so close to getting caught the first time that I knew I must learn to be in charge of my emotions or I was going to be in big trouble. I taught myself how to calm down when I wanted to kill somebody for anything that I considered an insult. I knew that someday, some place and somehow, I would get even with my offenders.

I was a junior in high school when my family went on a two-week vacation in Florida. While I was gone one of my best friends, Tony Thomas, went to a school dance and hooked up with Pat Bergman, who I was dating, and they made out. The hickeys were still showing when I got back home so there was no denying what had happened. They never apologized to me. It took days before I settled down enough that I could even face them without wanting to kill them right there on the spot. I swore that someday I would get even.

And, I did. Ten years later at our class reunion, I killed Pat and Tony. I'm sure it's a shame that a nice old woman had to be eliminated before I could make that happen.

Let's back up just a little.

After I graduated from high school I attended DePaul University in Chicago, my major being business administration. Right after graduating from college, I interviewed for a job with a consulting firm. I was hired and started at the bottom. Over the next ten years, I moved up to general manager, which was a pretty big deal with this company. I was making good money, I was more than comfortable, and I had a good life. My position required that I do a great deal of travel and I was probably out of the office more than in.

It had been ten years since I had left high school and the kids I went to school with were long forgotten. So, when I received a notice that our high school class was celebrating its ten-year reunion my first instinct was to throw the invitation in the garbage and forget about going. Then Pat and Tony slowly surfaced from the depths of my brain and my heart started to pound. Would I ever get a better chance to finally take revenge on a couple of traitors? Probably not. And, they would never see it coming.

I sent my response with a check back to Paul, the chairman of the reunion committee, adding a note that said I wouldn't miss it for the world.

A couple of classmates dying on the same night at the same time would definitely be suspicious. I couldn't just stand up and shoot them, so I needed to get inventive. The reunion was four months away and I spent most of that time coming up with a plan on how to kill and not be caught.

There is probably nothing you can't find on the internet, and I searched the deadly poison websites for hours. I learned about belladonna, cyanide, arsenic, hemlock, and the list went on and on. Some were fast-acting and some took days or weeks. All were detectable.

Then I came across an article on the Doll's Eye plant. It wasn't in the top ten poisons list or even the top twenty. The article stated that this plant was the cause of a few deaths a year, as the fruit is sweet and often mistaken for a type of berry. It was usually little kids who ate the berries by mistake and died. And the best part—it was readily available for purchase in the United States. This might just work.

I proceeded to order a Bunsen burner, some beakers, and other lab supplies that I thought I might need. I ordered the Doll's Eye plants from a mail-order nursery in Minnesota, making sure I ordered enough so I wouldn't run out and have to reorder. One order would be normal. More than that might become suspicious. I was about to become a mad scientist.

My next step was to find a pet store that sold mice, which was easy enough. There is a demand for mice, not only as little dumb pets but also from owners of snakes. I understand that a little mouse once a week or so keeps their snakes fed and full. I went shopping and bought a dozen of these little creatures, figuring that should be enough. I bought a cage to house them for the short time they would be with me.

The packages with the lab supplies arrived a few days later. I had set up a makeshift lab in a spare room in my apartment. I had a table by the window to put the plants on. I added another small table for the lab supplies. The third table held the cage with the mice. They were dirty little things and I had already cleaned their cage several times, as mice piss could make a room smell pretty bad in a short period of time.

I had read that the entire Doll's Eye plant is poisonous. The fruit of the plant or the 'eye' is where most of the toxins are concentrated. If ingested the toxin will have an immediate effect on the heart muscles and will cause a swift death mimicking heart failure. Perfect.

I planned to take the fruit of the plant and make it into a powder. The mice would be turned into guinea pigs on which to test the poison. Once I had perfected it--well, goodbye Pat and Tony forever.

How hard could it be?

"And, was it? Dr. Miller interrupted.

I was lying on his couch telling my story. My eyes snapped open at the sound of his voice and I looked at him. I had almost forgotten he was there. I had been talking for almost an hour now without any interruptions and the sound of his voice after all this time surprised me. "I'm sorry, what did you say?"

"Hard. How hard was it to make the powder?"

I was quiet for a minute as I thought about his question. "You know, it was easy to make but kind of hard to test. There's a big difference between killing a mouse and killing a person. But I'd have to say it wasn't that difficult to make at all."

I suddenly felt extremely tired and I told Dr. Miller that I was done for the day and wanted to leave.

He asked if I could stay for another half hour and finish my story. He also said he had some questions for me. I said no, I was wiped out. I stood up, shook his hand, and left.

Six

On the ride home from my appointment with Dr. Miller, I thought about the people I had killed over the years. I had absolutely no regrets. It was unfortunate that a few people had lost their lives along the way, but as the saying goes, 'that's the price of doing business.'

Now I was dying of brain cancer and I would be gone in a few months. Some people would probably say it was payback. I figured that it was just the circle of life. I had been told by Dr. Fuller that as the cancer progressed, I would probably experience memory loss, impaired judgment, seizures, and headaches. So far, all I was experiencing were headaches and I'm not sure that they were caused by the brain tumor. I'd had headaches most of my life.

I was sixty years old and I had devoted thirty of those years to my job. I was glad that I had retired young and spent some of the past seven years traveling. It was gratifying that my parents were gone and didn't have to watch me suffer during the last few months of my life. I didn't know if there was an afterlife. Perhaps, perhaps not. I hoped there was because that meant that one day I would be with Quinn.

I was ready to die.

I pulled into my driveway and just sat there, feeling so worn out I didn't even want to get out of the car. I was getting more tired each day. It was important that I finish these sessions with Dr. Miller as soon as possible. Perhaps I should stay longer than an hour if that's what he wants and just get it over with.

Seven

I cooked the 'eyes' and let them dry out. Once they were completely dry, I put them into a mortar. Then, using the matching pestle, I mashed them into fine powder. Wearing surgical gloves, I carefully picked out any larger pieces that remained and discarded them.

I placed a small shoebox on the table and I put a small piece of cheese in the box. I added just a smidgen of the powder to the top of the cheese.

I took the fattest mouse out of the cage and set him in the shoebox next to the cheese. He gobbled it up like a starving child, turned his head, and looked at me as if to say, "May I have some more, please."

I expected immediate results even though I had only put an extremely small amount of the powder on the cheese. I watched him for the next five or ten minutes and nothing happened. I tossed him back in the cage with his friends and left the room. I disposed of the gloves and decided to do some grocery shopping.

As I did my shopping, I considered using a different approach for making the powder. Perhaps I needed to mash the 'eyes' before I cooked them or cook them less. I needed to get the right formula, as time was now becoming an issue. The reunion was getting closer and I needed to know that my poison was going to work. I finished shopping, returned home, put the groceries away, and went to check on the mouse.

I glanced at the cage as I entered the room. Crap. The fat mouse was down for the count but now I knew why she was so fat. Seven little ugly hairless baby mice were trying to feed off her dead nipples. The poison had worked but it had taken longer than I expected it to. I considered that it might have been because she was pregnant. Whatever the reason, it took long enough that she managed to give birth before she died.

I threw the mother mouse and her babies into a garbage bag, walked down the hallway to the trash slot, and threw it in. Back in my apartment, I started experimenting with the powder.

Throughout the afternoon, each mouse died and each died a little faster. The last mouse had barely swallowed his cheese before he dropped over. The next step was to find out how much it would take to kill a person and how fast the powder would work. I needed one more test subject and it needed to be one walking on two legs.

Elsie Montie lived across the hall from me. She had moved into the building right after it had been built forty years ago. She was now a lonely old woman of eighty-six. I figured she had lived her life and should be ready to meet her maker. She had never married and had no children and I doubted that anyone would miss her or that there would be an autopsy. A heart attack would probably be listed as the cause of death.

Elsie and I had been friendly since I moved into my apartment four years ago. We occasionally had a cup of coffee with some of her homemade cookies. We would visit for a little while and she would tell me about her sad, long life. Most of her friends had either moved south or were dead. She seemed to be extremely lonely.

I ordered a pizza from Mik's and Carlo's Pizza and then went across the hall and knocked on Elsie's door. After she answered, I told her that I had ordered a pizza. I knew I wouldn't be able to eat it all and I asked her if she would like a few slices for her dinner. She was thrilled and I told her I would drop it off as soon as it was delivered. She asked if we could eat together and I said that would be great and that I would be over right after the pizza arrived.

It took about forty-five minutes before the pizza was delivered. I removed half the slices from the box and placed them on a paper plate. Then I carefully sprinkled some powder on the remaining pieces in the box. I placed those pieces on another paper plate and covered both plates with foil. I picked up the two plates of pizza, went back across the hall, and knocked on Elsie's apartment door.

Elsie was on her second slice when she looked up at me with a puzzled look on her face. Her death was quick. Her heart simply shut down and she was gone. There was no foaming at the mouth and she didn't have a seizure. She just grabbed at her chest and slumped over.

I was ready for my reunion.

"I think I'll stop here for now, Doctor. Do you have any questions for me today?"

"What did they say was the cause of her death?" he asked.

"Simple heart attack. After all, she was old. No one suspected anything. Why would they? I was just a neighbor having a few slices with her. It was a good thing I was there to call the paramedics, they said. Otherwise, who knew how long it would have been before someone found her." I replied.

"How did you feel after? Did you feel any remorse after killing her? After all, she hadn't harmed you and you were friends."

"Not really friends, just neighbors."

"Yes, but you had known her for four years. Surely, you must have had some regrets after poisoning her," the doctor said.

"She was an essential part of my experiment. I actually appreciated what she did for me. I needed a test subject and she was there. She gave me the answer I needed so I could prepare for my next two kills. Remorse? Of course not. But I did appreciate her help. Do you want me to continue or are we done for the day?"

"Please, let's continue for another half hour or so," he answered.

I cooked the remaining fruit from the rest of the Doll's Eyes plants and made them into powder. I had plenty of it now but I had no idea how long it would stay potent enough to kill. I hoped it would never lose its potency. If this worked as I hoped it would, I could continue to use this powder if and when necessary. Hitting people with a bat is messy and a gun is noisy. I liked what I had done.

I separated a Tylenol capsule over the sink, emptied the medication, and filled one of the halves with the powder. Then I put the two ends back together. Perfect. This worked exactly as I wanted it to.

Piece by piece I disposed of everything that I had purchased to use in my make-shift lab. I took the mouse cage, the unused parts of the plants and the pots they came in, and put them into a large black garbage bag. The Bunsen burner and beakers followed and I put everything in the trash. The only thing that remained when I was finished cleaning up was a small container, which held the remaining powder.

I emptied another eleven Tylenol capsules, carefully filled them with the remaining powder, and put them into a plastic sandwich bag. Then, just to be safe, I double-bagged the pills and put them in my wall safe.

Now I just needed to make my reservation, at a motel in my old hometown, and go shopping for some new clothes. I didn't need much, as I knew the reunion would be casual and most of the people there would probably be in shorts or jeans.

There was a good turnout and it was a fun night. I saw friends I hadn't seen in years and we caught up on each other lives. Most of them were married and had little kids. It didn't surprise me that many of them were still living in the same town they had grown up in or just a short distance from it. I had traveled the world and except for a few, most had never left Wisconsin.

About an hour into cocktails Paul, the chairman of the committee, announced that dinner was served. Most everyone was drinking and they brought their unfinished drinks with them to the tables. I had hooked up with Pat and Tony at the bar and we decided to sit together at the same table so we could continue our conversation.

The waitresses had already placed our salads on the table so we started eating as soon as we sat down. They would also be serving us our dessert and coffee. The main course was set up buffet style and we had a choice of ham, beef, or chicken. Paul joked as he told us that the committee couldn't agree as to what type of meat to serve, so they decided to have it all. Everyone would have to leave the table after they finished their salads to get their meat and sides. I couldn't have planned it any better.

Pat and Tony had both brought their unfinished drinks to the table. I ate slowly so when they got up to get their main course, I was just finishing my salad. As soon as they left the table, I looked around to see if anyone was watching. Almost everyone was heading up to the buffet table anxious to eat. Knowing I may not have a better chance than right then, I reached into my pocket and took out the capsule. In less than five seconds, I opened it and had sprinkled a very small amount of powder into each of their drinks.

I learned while experimenting with the mice that almost any amount would kill a person. I had also learned that the smaller the amount the longer it took to do its job. I figured Tony and Pat would probably die on their way home a few hours from now.

Tony lived in a neighboring town that was fifteen miles away. They found the wrecked car wrapped around a tree at approximately four am, with Tony dead inside. The authorities said the accident was due to being under the influence and losing control of the vehicle.

Pat wasn't quite so lucky. Being a lot heavier than Tony, it took longer for the poison to work. Feeling dizzy shortly after getting home, Pat stepped out onto the sixth-floor balcony of the apartment to get some fresh air, tripped, and fell hard against the railing, knocking it loose. Pat went over the side and fell six floors before being impaled on the black wrought iron fence finials below.

The next morning, I checked out of the motel I was staying at and drove to a local diner for breakfast. It was buzzing with the news of the two deaths. It was sad, people were saying, the way Tony died, but Pat's death was gruesome. I could barely keep from smiling when I heard someone say that it took three men over an hour to lift Pat off that fence in one piece.

I left the diner after finishing my meal and drove back to Chicago thinking that the food wasn't that good but it was definitely one hell of a class reunion. I was feeling good.

"So, that makes four people you've murdered. How many more, Sydney, before this ends?"

I ignored his question. "I have a doctor's appointment tomorrow. I won't make my four o'clock with you." I told him. "We'll pick it up on Wednesday, okay?"

"Seeing your oncologist?" He asked.

"It never ends. I'll see you then," I replied.

Eight

I started working at L&L Consulting when I graduated from college. Mr. Lilly, who was my boss and co-owner of the company, was an extremely religious man. It was a requirement that his employees have high moral standards. You never heard swearing or dirty jokes from anyone while working. Mr. Lilly wasn't a total prude, but anyone who slipped up could expect to be called in for a reminder that such language was not to be used in or around the office. No one worked on Sunday and he forbade anyone to come into the office on that day. Sunday was meant for his employees to go to church and spend time with their families. That rule meant that a lot of us took work home if we had projects that needed to be completed. We often put in a seven-day workweek without Mr. Lilly ever knowing about it.

Mr. Little, Mr. Lilly's partner, was a little less demanding than his partner was. Even so, every employee had to sign a contract that included a moral clause with the understanding that if we fucked up, we were gone. We represented their company and they insisted that they be represented with the highest moral standards possible.

I played their game and, shortly after moving to Chicago and going to work for L&L Consulting, I found a church. Church and religion weren't new to me. My parents had raised my siblings and me in the church and we could be found sitting in a pew most Sunday mornings. When I wasn't traveling, I usually attended church and listened to Rev. Rob Meyer give a sermon. I didn't particularly care for him and some of his sermons pissed me off. However, I obtained the necessary information to have something to discuss when Mr. Lilly would ask me, on Monday morning, if I had enjoyed church the day before.

I had been in Vienna, Austria for a few years helping start up a new branch office. I traveled back to the States every few months to check-in and update Mr. Lilly and Mr. Little on the progress we were making. Now the new office was ready to be turned over to the manager and I was headed home. This had definitely been one of the happier times in my life and I was sorry to leave Vienna. It's a beautiful city and when I wasn't working, I was sightseeing.

I got off the plane, tired and short-tempered. The flight had been rough making it impossible to get any sleep on the way home. I finally made it to my apartment, opened the door, fell into bed, and within minutes I was sound asleep.

The next day I went across the hall to my neighbor's apartment to retrieve my mail from Mike, who had been collecting it for me while I was gone. I expected to find just the usual junk mail, as Mike had instructions to call me if anything looked important.

Tucked in with all that junk mail, there was a letter

from my church, which had been sent bulk mail. Obviously, Mike hadn't given it a second thought, as it didn't look important. I opened it. I read it. And, I saw red.

The letter notified me that I had been dropped as a member of my church for not living up to my pledge and fulfilling my financial obligation. I had told Rev. Meyer that I would be in Austria and asked if I could put a hold on my membership. He wanted to transfer me to a different church but I said no, as I intended to come back. It seemed the finance committee or the church secretary had not been given this information and someone recommended that I be dropped as a member. Rev. Meyer, who made the final decision on who to keep and who to eliminate, had written me off after thirteen years of being a member of my church.

He knew I intended to continue after I returned from Austria. It was all about the money. I was so pissed I could hardly see straight.

It was obvious that Rev. Meyer had to pay and I wasn't about to wait ten years to get revenge.

It took me a few days to settle down and start to think with a cool head.

"You killed a minister?" Dr. Miller interrupted me. "You actually killed a man of the cloth?"

"Don't you get it? Almost every Monday morning, since I had started working at L&L, my boss asked if I enjoyed church and what the sermon had been about. How was I going to now tell my boss that I couldn't go to church because I'd been kicked out? Of a church! No matter what I said, it would look bad. This man of the cloth, as you call him, could have easily destroyed my life."

"It just seems a little extreme, that's all. I mean, certainly your boss would understand that it wasn't your fault."

"I wasn't about to risk it."

"So, your answer was to just kill him?'

"He pissed me off and he deserved what he got. Do you have any idea how embarrassing this was? Church people gossip, you know. I could hear them in my head. Laughing about me. Making fun of me. I couldn't just let that go. Why can't you understand that? I was the injured party here, not him."

"I'm trying to understand, that's all. Sorry, I interrupted you, Sydney. Please continue," he replied.

I actually did cool down and decided I should confront Rev. Meyer before I did anything stupid. I was no longer twelve years old.

I thought perhaps I could talk to him and work this problem out so I called him at the church office. His secretary answered the phone and I asked to speak to him. She put me on hold. A few seconds later, she was back on the line and told me that he was not in the office. Bullshit! I asked her when he would be back and was told that he wouldn't be in until the next day.

I put on my coat, left my apartment, and took the elevator down to the basement where my car was parked. I drove the mile and a half to the church and pulled into the parking lot at two-thirty pm. There were only two other cars in the lot and both were parked close to the church office entrance. I was about to park next to one of the cars when I saw Rev. Meyer walk out of the building and head toward his car. As soon as his feet touched the parking lot pavement, I hit the gas pedal as hard as I could. The car went flying forward and hit him straight on. The impact threw him forward and he hit the pavement hard. I backed the car up, threw it into forward, and proceeded to run over him.

I took off out of the parking lot and drove down the street. After driving a few blocks, I pulled over into a vacant lot and stopped. I turned the car off and just sat there shaking and laughing. I was afraid and, at the same time, I was in heaven. The bastard was dead. He had to be dead. His head had been my target and there was no way he could have survived.

Well, so much for control. My life was probably over as I knew it. I sat there for the next few minutes and settled down. I was sure this time I would be caught. I didn't care what happened to me or if I was caught. Right then—in that minute—I only cared about how I felt. I can't put that feeling into words. It was kind of like I was outside my body looking down in wonder at the most amazing person in the world and it felt glorious.

I left the vacant lot and headed back toward my apartment. As I approached the intersection where my building was located, I purposely rear-ended a car that was slowing down for a traffic light. I was hoping that the impact would cover any damage that had been done to my car when I ran down Rev. Meyer. A traffic ticket would be a small price to pay for what I had just done. Suddenly, I was rear-ended by the car behind me. The impact threw me forward and my head hit the steering wheel knocking me out. If the airbags had deployed, I would probably have been okay but my front impact hadn't been hard enough to make that happen.

I woke up in the paramedics' van. Of course, the police were on the scene trying to determine who was at fault. They finally determined that the car behind me had caused the accident. I sat and waited until the accident report was completed and the driver that had been behind me was ticketed. The tow truck showed up and I watched while my car was towed away.

I declined a trip to the hospital and was told that if I started to display any symptoms of a concussion, I should see a doctor immediately. I thanked everyone for being so nice and walked into my apartment building.

The notice of Rev. Rob Meyer's death was the first story on the six o'clock news. His secretary found him lying on the pavement when she left work at five. Although he was unresponsive, he was transported to Chicago Memorial Hospital where he was pronounced DOA. She told the investigators that Rev. Meyer had left his office around three or so and she had not seen or heard anything after he left. The security cameras were set to come on after dark so there was no video to watch.

At three o'clock, I was in a car accident one and a half miles away from the church with a police officer as my witness.

There is no question that I had lucked out once again. If the church secretary had looked at the clock and had known exactly what time Rev. Meyer left the church, I might have been caught. If the security cameras turned on a little sooner, I might have been caught. I had been reckless and I had let my temper take over and win against patience and planning. I had committed another bloody violent crime.

My car had some serious damage, especially to the back end. I had no intention of having it repaired, so I sold it for parts to a body shop. I wanted it destroyed and out of my sight.

The next Saturday I went car shopping and treated myself to a new beautiful black Infinity Q45 sedan.

I did my best to steer clear of the topic of church for a

while. A few weeks later, when my boss, Mr. Lilly, asked me about the Sunday sermon, I simply told him I had changed churches. He seemed somewhat surprised but was happy that I had found a new home where I could worship.

"Why didn't you just do that in the first place? Rather than running your pastor over with your car, why didn't you just change churches? It seems a little unreasonable to me that you would be afraid to tell your boss that you had made a move to a different church." Dr. Miller inquired.

"Well, I didn't plan to kill him like that. When I saw him walking to his car, I didn't even think about what I was going to do. I just did it. He kicked me out of my church and that was totally unacceptable. I don't think I could have changed churches and just ignored him. Eventually, one way or the other, he was going to die. I just didn't plan on it being there in the parking lot. I was so angry when I saw him walk out of that building I couldn't see straight. He pissed me off and he suffered the consequences. I don't think you get it, Doctor." I was yelling now. Dr. Miller was starting to piss me off.

"I'm trying to understand this feeling that comes over you, Sydney. Please don't misunderstand me when I ask you these questions. I'm just trying to – "

"What?" I interrupted. You're judging me. I don't like to be judged. Or, do you think you're going to cure me? I told you, I can't help what I do. I can't control it. I'm not here to be helped. I'm here to tell you my story so that you can tell the FBI after I die. Let's not get distracted by your need to delve into my psyche. I'm not going to be cured of my cancer and you're certainly not going to cure my obsession to kill."

It was our fifth session. I was tired and most of the time I was living with a bad headache. Things were starting to aggravate me more and more and I was snapping at people over the slightest little thing. I took a deep breath and tried to settle down.

"Doctor, it's these damn headaches. They're making me crazy. I realize it's hard for you to listen and not say anything. I'm taking a few days off but I'll be back on Monday for our regular appointment."

"Oh, are you going away?"

"No. I'm starting a new medication for my headaches. I've been told that it's going to be trial and error over the next few days in order to get the right dosage. Hopefully, I'll be in a better state of mind when I see you Monday."

"Tell me, Sydney, are your headaches worse than when you first started seeing me?"

"They are probably about the same, which means they are still really bad," I replied.

"Well, I hope, for your sake, that this new medication helps. See you on Monday."

Nine

When Dr. Fuller, my oncologist, told me that I would be sleeping a lot over the next few days, she was right on the money. Between Wednesday and Saturday, I was asleep more than awake. I checked in with her each day and by Saturday we were starting to see some good results. I was not experiencing the same degree of mind-blowing pain in my head and I was sleeping less. Sunday night I had a normal night's sleep and woke up ready and anxious for my appointment with Dr. Miller the next afternoon.

I was in Dr. Miller's waiting room and it was a little after four. Dr. Miller was a stickler for being on time so I figured I would be seen soon. Another ten minutes went by and I still had not been called into his office. Finally, after waiting thirty minutes past my scheduled appointment the door from his office to the waiting room opened and Dr. Miller asked me to join him.

"So, what's up Doc? You're never late," I said as I got up off my chair and walked into his office.

"I'm extremely sorry, Sydney. I have a patient who was basically having a melt down and I needed to spend a little extra time with him."

"So, did using my time fix him?"

"Some people will never be fixed no matter how much time you spend with them," Dr. Miller said. "But it did help.

Thanks for waiting. I hate it when I don't run on schedule and I'll try to be sure you won't need to wait again."

"I would appreciate that very much."

"So, Sydney, do you mind if I ask how your weekend went? Are you finding that the new medication is working?"

"I would say that over the past few days, the intensity of my headaches has lessened by about seventy-five percent. This new drug, Sildapederoryacin, is still in the testing stage and my oncologist only got me into a test group because I'm dying. There is some talk about also testing it on people who have migraine headaches. They figure if this helps cancer patients, it might also help them. You might want to pick up a few shares of their stock, as this is going to be big if it gets approved."

"Thanks for the tip, I'll look into it. Ready to start?"

"You know, Doc, I'd like to talk about something else today. It's about a dream I keep having."

"Really? Get comfortable and tell me about it."

I decided on the couch today. I settled in on it and started. "I'm little, maybe five or six, but I'm much taller than anyone in my family. I'm on a swing and when I'm high in the sky I become really, really little but the swing stays the same size. When the swing comes back down, I'm big again. Then all of a sudden, I'm back to normal size and I'm on a merry-go-round. Not like at a carnival, but the old-fashioned ones that we used to have on school playgrounds. My father is pushing it and it goes faster and faster until I can't make out anything and I can't see where my father is standing. Then I start to grow until I'm huge, like a giant. I jump off the merry-go-round, pick it up, and throw it at my father. Suddenly, he is bigger than me and he catches it. Then we are all normal again and he picks me up and holds me and tells me he'll never let me go. And, I wake up. My heart is racing and I'm dying of thirst."

All the while I have been talking the doctor has been making notes. I look at him, expecting to hear some earth-shattering news about what my dream means.

"Your sub-conscience is probably remembering when you were little and fell off a swing. You were powerless when that happened. Now you want the power. Being bigger and towering over everyone puts you in charge and in control. Even at a young age, you were ready to fight your father for the power, even if it meant destroying him. At the same time, you want to be normal and loved by your father and have him take care of you," Dr. Miller tells me.

"But I loved my father. We always had a great relationship. He was one of the most thoughtful caring men I ever met. Why would I want to destroy someone who always loved me and was my biggest supporter?" I ask.

"Think about it Sydney. You have always felt the need to be on top and in control of any situation and the people who surround you. You won't and haven't let anyone or anything stand in your way. This anger you feel that you say you can't control is probably caused because someone tried to take control for a short time and you can't have that so you need to strike back. Perhaps, you did have some brain damage when you were small and that is the reason for what you have done or maybe it's just the way you were born. We will probably never know for sure."

"Then again, Doc, we just might. I want my brain donated to the Department of Psychology at the University of Chicago after I die so it can be studied. Can you set that up for me?"

"You're serious?"

"Why not? In some small way, it may help someone if they find that a fall I had when I was young caused some brain damage. Perhaps that's why I am like I am. I know I'm not normal, Doctor Miller. I've seen how people react over the loss of loved ones. I've lost both my parents and a brother and I never felt any type of real loss. I learned how to fake it years ago. People get angry and upset and get over it. I have to destroy someone to get over my anger. Don't you think it would help to have them at least take a look?"

"Sydney, I already know what is wrong with you. You are a psychopath. Do you know what that means?'

"No way! You know why? Because I can love. I loved my family and years ago I fell in love. Very much in love. Psychopaths can't express love. I've read the books. You're wrong."

"Sydney, there are exceptions to every rule. You have enough of the symptoms to be diagnosed as a psychopath. I'm sorry if that's not what you want to hear, but it's the truth."

"Well, you're wrong, doctor. Very wrong," I said.

"I don't want to dwell on this as it's not important for why you are here," Dr. Miller said. "As I said, there are exceptions and each individual is different. I believe you believe you once fell in love, as we all have our own perception of what love is."

"You know, doctor, sometimes I wonder if you know what the fuck you are talking about."

"Please, Sydney, don't get upset. We're just talking here, doctor and patient. I'm sure you have loved. I could be wrong. Let's just continue and forget we ever talked about this."

"You know, doc, it's really hard for me to forget stuff. Anyway, it's past five and I should be going. My medication is sitting on my kitchen counter and it's time for a pill."

"Take care. I'll see you tomorrow," Dr. Miller said as I walked out the door, thinking that there were times when he really could piss me off.

Ten

Approximately six months after the death of Rev. Meyer, Mr. Lilly informed me that I had been selected to set up a branch office in Limerick, Ireland. I was thrilled. I wasn't concerned about being away from family and friends for a few years. The job would have me commuting between Ireland and Chicago every few months and I would see my family and friends when I was back in the States.

On the other hand, even though the investigation into the Reverend's death had gone cold, it was still an open case. I figured it wouldn't hurt if I was out of Chicago for a while.

I decided to rent out my apartment rather than have it sit empty for a few years. I placed an ad on the internet with an apartment rental agency and was surprised at how many responses it got. After numerous interviews, I found a nice couple, Rodney and Missy Brown, and rented them my apartment. They assured me they would look after it and treat it like their own. I had run a credit check on them and felt secure with my decision to rent to them. When I was back in Chicago for a few days during this time, I just stayed with friends or settled into a hotel.

By now, L&L Consulting had grown considerably and had offices all over the world. Limerick was the second overseas office I set up and working with the easy-going Irish made it fun and easy. In no time at all, new clients were at our door and we got busier every week. I hired the best people possible and my job was to train them and oversee the day-to-day operation. My bosses needed to be confident that, when I left Limerick and went back home, the office would continue to run smoothly.

My job was demanding and I worked my butt off, but I loved what I was doing and didn't mind the long hours I had to put in. Just like in the States, no one was supposed to work in any office that belonged to L&L on Sundays. Once I felt comfortable leaving the office in the hands of the new employees for a day or two, I took long weekends and started exploring Ireland. I traveled all over the country, fascinated at the difference between the red-haired Irish people who live in the eastern part of the country near Dublin and the dark-haired Irish of Limerick, which was nearer to the west side of Ireland. I traveled to Wales, Scotland, and England. I soaked up the beauty of the countryside and learned about the different cultures of these countries.

I had added King John's Castle to my list of places to visit before I left to go back home. It's located in Limerick next to the River Shannon and was just a short drive from my apartment. On a sunny Sunday, I took the tour, which included drinking a little mead and enjoying a medieval feast, which we ate with our fingers.

Driving home after the tour, I decided to stop at O'Shaughnessy's Pub for a drink. Standing at the end of the bar was the most stunning person I have ever seen. Ninety minutes later, we were back in my apartment fucking our heads off.

I'd had a few short-lived affairs before I met Quinn McGuire. I enjoyed being with the opposite sex but eventually I would just get bored and move on. My job took up a great deal of my time and I never found anyone that tempted me to put the time into a relationship to make it work. I knew it was better to love 'em and leave 'em, as the saying goes. So, at the age of thirty-seven, I had never had what most people would call a serious relationship.

Quinn, however, took me to another level and brought out feelings I didn't know existed. I was so much in love I could hardly see straight and we spent every possible minute together. I was under a spell and I hoped that spell would never be broken.

Quinn had been born and raised in Dublin. After we had been seeing each other for almost three months we decided I should meet the rest of the McGuire family. We drove to Dublin and spent the weekend, having been told right up front that we would not be sharing a room. Quinn's parents were strict Catholics and there would be no shenanigans in their house.

They were a fun-loving family, though, and I could understand why Quinn was such a happy, fun-loving person.

We knew my time in Limerick was coming to an end

and it wouldn't be long before I would have to return to the States. Quinn and I discussed all our options and we decided I should stay in Ireland for good. I knew I couldn't live without Quinn. I was going to ask my boss if I could stay on and run the new office in Limerick.

Three weeks later, I was called back to Chicago for a meeting with Mr. Lilly. We discussed turning the Limerick office over to the new manager and the timeline for my permanent return to Chicago. Before I had the chance to ask if I could run the Limerick office Mr. Lilly informed me that he had some great news. I was getting a huge promotion and a salary increase. I would be making the high side of six figures if I took his offer. It also meant that my traveling days would pretty much end and I would spend most of my time working in the Chicago office. I had been waiting for this offer for years. I couldn't leave Chicago.

It didn't take long to come up with an alternative plan. Quinn could move to Chicago instead of me staying in Limerick. I'd sell my apartment and buy us a larger place to live. I wondered about the availability and prices of an apartment on the lake. I knew they were expensive but I could afford it. I was sure Quinn would love living in Chicago in a home on Lake Michigan.

I was leaving to go back to Ireland in a few days and I waited until I got back to discuss the change in plans. It took a lot of convincing, as Quinn didn't want to leave Ireland, but we finally agreed that settling in Chicago was probably the best way to go and that it didn't matter where we lived, as long as we were together.

A couple of weeks later, I packed up my belongings and headed home to Chicago. We figured it would take at least four weeks before Quinn would be able to join me. Saying goodbye was the hardest thing I'd ever done.

My renters, Rodney and Sissy Brown, had not paid the rent for the apartment for the last three months. They had a six-month lease which had been renewed every six months since I had been gone. However, I had a stipulation in the lease that, with a sixty-day notice, I could ask them to vacate the apartment. I had been trying for almost two months to contact them to let them know that I would be back and that they needed to make arrangements to move. I had not heard from them, so I sent them a certified letter requesting they call me. They never responded to my letter.

I had intended to stop at the apartment the last time I was in Chicago. But, with the news of the promotion, I was so anxious to get on that plane and back to Quinn that I let it slide.

I arrived home hoping that they would be willing to leave without having to get an eviction notice. I certainly didn't want any problems. There was no answer when I knocked on the door, so I took out my key and unlocked it. I opened the door and walked into an empty, trashed apartment with toilets full of crap, closet doors hanging off their hinges and you could barely tell what color the carpet had been. The place stunk to high heaven. I was so mad I could hardly breathe.

I stepped out into the hall, took a deep breath, and knocked on Mike's door. An elderly man answered. I told him who I was and asked for Mike. He told me that Mike no longer lived there. He had sold his apartment while I was gone. I asked him if he knew where the Browns had gone and he told me they had moved out about three months ago. He didn't know where they had gone, muttered good riddance under his breath, and asked when I was going to do something about getting rid of the smell coming from my place.

I apologized to him and explained that I had been out of the country and I would get it taken care of soon. During our short conversation, he told me that the Browns had at least six or seven other people living there with them. He also said that he was pretty sure, because of the tee-shirts they were always wearing, that some of them worked at a restaurant near the train station on South Canal Street. I thanked him, locked up the apartment, and left.

Once in my car, I called an extended-stay motel and made a reservation, telling them I would probably be staying there for at least two or three months. I Googled cleaning services and found a company that specialized in cleaning up disaster scenes. I called them and scheduled a time for them to clean my apartment.

I drove to the motel and settled in. Once I was unpacked, I called a contractor who specialized in home repairs and scheduled an appointment to meet the next day. I needed to get an estimate as to what it would cost to get my apartment back in shape. I couldn't even think about putting it on the market until it was presentable.

My adrenalin was pumping and I wanted to punch something. I took a long hot shower and tried to settle down. It had been a long flight and it had been a bad day. I was pissed and, even though I was tired, I couldn't sleep. I lay there planning my revenge and the first step was to find the Browns.

"This might be a good place to stop for today, Sydney," Dr. Miller said.

Once again, the sound of his voice startled me and brought me back to reality. I opened my eyes and sat up. "Yes, you're right. The rest of this story is going to take a while."

Eleven

I barely slept that night and I was up early. I put on a pot of coffee, watched the morning news, and took a shower. At eight o'clock sharp, I called Mr. Lilly. He picked up on the first ring and I explained to him what had happened with my apartment and that I needed a week off. I must have sounded extremely stressed as he readily agreed and told me to take as much time as I needed.

I met with Jimmy Regan, the contractor, at nine-thirty. He walked from room and room making notes. He told me that there was so much damage that it would be easier to replace almost everything rather than try to fix it. Fixtures, cabinets, counter tops, flooring, and appliances needed to be replaced. The longer the list became, the more the dollars added up and the more agitated I became. I told him the cleaners would be in to clean the apartment the next day and asked him to write up the contract. As soon as I received it, he could start work, and the sooner the better. I just wanted to get this fixed and I wasn't going to start messing around with getting two or three more estimates. I had other more important matters to attend to.

It was now afternoon and I still hadn't talked to Quinn. It would be around six in Ireland and Quinn would probably be having dinner. I placed the call and was sent to voice mail. I would try later.

I drove to Isaacson's Storage Lockers and parked outside one of the two lockers I had rented before leaving for Ireland. I had to think for a minute before I remembered which locker I had stored the box with the Doll's Eye powder. The powder was now a little more than ten years old and I had no idea if it would still do the trick and I needed to find out.

Then I remembered 'five, six, pick up sticks'. It was the other locker. Locker fifty-six. I drove the short distance to locker fifty-six, got out of the car, and opened it. The box was up front so I didn't have to start digging to find it. I put the box in my car, closed up the locker, and drove back to the motel.

Ten years ago, I had filled twelve capsules with poison and eleven remained. I opened the sandwich bags, dumped the capsules onto the coffee table, and then put ten back. One would be enough for now.

I tried calling Quinn again and again my call went to voice mail. It was night there so I would try again tomorrow, although it was strange that my calls weren't being returned.

There are thousands of people named Brown living in Chicago and over a hundred with the first name of Rodney. I wondered how the hell I was going to find Rodney and Missy Brown. Plan it out, I told myself. One step at a time.

I decided to follow up on my neighbor's comment regarding the shirts some of the people who nested in my apartment wore and I headed for the B and L Diner. I parked across the street and watched the customers come and go, most of them taking around thirty minutes to order, eat, and leave. Fast service, I thought. Then Missy Brown walked out the door and headed up the street. My heart started to pound. My car was parked facing the opposite direction and I knew I would lose her if I tried to follow her in my car. I got out and started walking behind her on the opposite side of the street. She turned the corner and went into River Heights Bank. I stood across the street watching the door while she did her banking. She came out a few minutes later and walked back to the diner. Now I knew where she worked but I needed to find out where she lived.

I decided to drive back to the motel, freshen up, and get something to eat. I felt a lot better after I showered and changed my clothes. By now, I was starving and more than ready for dinner. I took the elevator up to the restaurant where you could get anything from a hamburger to a steak. I chose a table close to an elderly gentleman and when the waitress came over and took my order, I opted for a Reuben sandwich with fries.

I had ordered a drink and was enjoying that while waiting for my meal. I decided to make my move, got up from the table, and headed to the washroom. As I passed the elderly gentleman, I tripped and started to fall. I grabbed his table to catch myself from falling and spilled his water all over his lap and the table. I apologized, picked up a napkin from an empty table next to him, and started wiping up the water. As I patted the table, he was busy wiping the water off his lap and, with absolutely no effort whatsoever, I emptied a capsule of powder into his coffee.

I apologized again and continued to the washroom. Then I returned to my table and ate a very good Rueben sandwich while watching the neighboring diner enjoy his last cup of coffee.

He never paid his final tab. The poison had worked.

"Why didn't you just wait to use the powder on the Browns? Was it really necessary to kill some old man?" Once again, Dr. Miller interrupted my train of thought to ask me a question.

"I think it's obvious. When I made my move on the Browns, I wanted to be sure it would work. I had one shot. Do you think I would have killed that old man if it hadn't been necessary? I don't just go around killing people for no reason. Yes, it was necessary. If it hadn't been him, it would have been someone else. Better to experiment on the elderly who have already lived their lives than young ones, don't you think?"

"Actually, I think it would have been better not to experiment or kill anyone. But we're not talking about me, here. Please continue. What happened next?"

"Fucking right, we're not talking about you and once again, Doctor, it sounds like you're being judgmental."

"Sorry, not at all. Please, continue."

For the next two days, I watched the diner and Mr. and Mrs. Brown. They catered to the breakfast and lunch crowd. The diner was open from six to three every day except Sunday, the only day it was closed. When Mrs. Brown left the diner on the second day, I followed her. She drove to a small home nestled between a couple of three-story buildings that housed stores on the lower level and apartments on the upper two floors. I watched her park her car in front and enter the house. I drove to the end of the block, turned around, and parked a few buildings down from her house, where I had a good view of the front door.

After about an hour or so, Mr. Brown pulled up in a brand-new Lincoln, parked behind his wife's car, and went into the house. During the next hour, I watched four more people, who I guessed were between the ages of sixteen to twenty-five, enter the home. All were wearing t-shirts bearing the name of the restaurant.

I had been parked there long enough. It was getting dark and I didn't feel I needed to call attention to myself by staying there any longer. I started the car and drove back to the motel.

I was worried about Quinn and called again. For the

past two days, my calls had gone unanswered and I decided if we didn't connect now, I was going to call Quinn's parents. Once again, my call went to Quinn's voice mail.

I followed through and called Quinn's father, who answered the phone and told me that everything was fine. Quinn had made a last-minute decision to visit relatives in Belfast before leaving for the States and would be back in Dublin in a few days. The phone I'd been calling had been forgotten and was sitting in a charger on a dresser back in Limerick.

I slept a lot better that night having been reassured that Quinn was okay.

I stopped talking. Tears were rolling down my cheeks and I couldn't go on.

"Are you okay?" Dr. Miller asked. "What's going on, Sydney? What has upset you so much that you're crying?"

He handed me a Kleenex. Finally, after a short silence, I got up. "I've got to leave. I can't do this. I'll see you tomorrow," I said and started to walk out the door.

"Wait. Obviously, you're upset and we should talk about it. It's not good to keep things inside. Please, sit down so we can discuss this."

"Looks like I've got feelings after all, doesn't it? I told you. You don't know me at all. Right now, I just need to get the hell out of here."

Twelve

I made it to my car without totally losing it. Quinn had been gone for twenty-two years now and I still found it hard to talk or even think about it. I finally got myself under control and backed out of my parking spot.

As I headed out of the parking lot, a large black van pulled around me and cut me off. I pulled my car to the right to avoid being hit by their car and hit a light pole. I wasn't going that fast so it was more of a tap than a hit and I didn't think any damage had been done. I had barely missed hitting a woman who was walking to her car and had tripped and fallen trying to avoid being hit. I got out of my car, went over to her, and helped her up. I asked if she was okay and she said she wasn't sure.

"I got their plate number," she said.

"Excuse me?"

"I got their license plate number if you want it. They were definitely at fault here and if you need a witness, I will certainly be happy to help you out."

"I appreciate it," I told her, "but there's no damage to my car. The only damage was done to you and you seem to be okay."

"Well, I'm not sure about that. It looks like you have a few scratches where you hit that light pole. My side is really hurting and I'm probably going to have to see a doctor.

Perhaps, I'll need you as a witness. Let's just exchange some information and I'll look into who owns that license plate," she replied.

"You think you can track this down?" I asked.

"I know I can track it down. I'm a cop and I'll have that information before the day is over."

We exchanged information, including the plate number, and we parted ways. The scratches weren't that bad and I could have them buffed out at a body shop. As far as I was concerned, this little incident was over.

I was surprised when she called me a couple of hours later. I asked her how she was feeling and she said she was in a lot of pain and was going to see a doctor. After a little more small talk, she told me that she had run the license plate and it was registered to the FBI.

Thirteen

Dr. Miller and I had been talking for about ten minutes. It was my tenth appointment and the subject of his fee was being discussed for the first time since I had started seeing him.

"Exactly how much do I owe you?" I asked. "We're coming to the end of my third week of meeting with you and you haven't sent me a bill. What's the damage so far? Do I need to get a mortgage on my apartment?"

"Do you know, Sydney, that's the first time I've seen a smidgen of humor come from you. I was wondering if you even have a sense of humor."

"There isn't much to laugh about these days, Doc," I replied.

"Let me check with my office manager and have her get a bill ready. You can settle up on your way out today if that's what you want."

"Sounds good. So let me finish telling you about Quinn."

Quinn was in Belfast for almost a week. Due to a bad connection, we only spoke once and it was a short conversation. We worked out a time schedule and if everything went according to plan, we would be together in Chicago in three weeks. I could hardly contain my excitement.

From Belfast Quinn went back to Dublin, said goodbye to family one more time, and left for the airport to catch the flight to the Shannon airport. There was still some packing to do and some items to be put into storage, which would eventually be shipped to Chicago.

The commuter plane from Dublin to the Shannon Airport crashed ten minutes after takeoff. The plane lost an engine and the pilot lost control of the plane. It hit the ground nose first and exploded on impact. There were no survivors.

I flew back to Ireland for Quinn's funeral, which was held in Dublin. After a three-day wake with plenty of weeping and drinking, Quinn was put to rest for the last time. It's hard to remember exactly what transpired during those few days, as I was still reeling from my loss.

After the funeral, I left Dublin and took the train to Limerick. I certainly had no intentions of getting on a commuter plane after what had happened to Quinn. The train ride took a little over two hours. I watched the beautiful rolling green countryside go by and started to relax. It had been the worst week of my life.

After I arrived in Limerick, I visited our new office. It was doing much better than anticipated and the staff had already been increased by two new employees. I visited with some old friends for a while and that night a few of us went to the pub. I got absolutely shit-faced and I still don't know who took me back to my hotel and tucked me in. I never asked and no one ever brought it up.

"I'm so sorry, Sydney. I had no idea. I'm sorry for your loss," Dr. Miller said.

"It was twenty-two years ago and it still seems like yesterday. Quinn was the only person I ever truly loved and the only person that gave my life meaning. The day that Quinn died, so did I. I contemplated suicide for a long time after that, but I guess I just didn't have the guts to follow through," I replied.

I went back to the States and back to work. When I wasn't working, I was planning. The Browns had not been forgotten.

My apartment was coming along nicely and Jimmy was doing a great job. He told me he figured it would take a couple more weeks to finish the remodeling. I decided to stay at the motel until the job was completed and then move back to the apartment. There was no need to buy a larger place now that Quinn was gone.

Three weeks later I hired some movers and had my belongings moved from the two storage lockers to my apartment. I took a long weekend to get settled in. Jimmy had done a fantastic job and I felt like I was in a brand-new home. I enjoyed the smell of fresh paint each time I walked through the front door. I had known what the repair cost was before the job was started and I had already paid almost half of it. I paid the balance I owed Jimmy, still festering at what the Browns had done. Now it was time to settle the Brown's debt to me. They had cost me over ninety thousand dollars.

As I did my unpacking, I found a box that held some of my important papers. Among them were the references the Browns had given me along with the application that they had filled out before I rented them my apartment. Three years ago, they ran a Dollar Store and were making a decent living. They had claimed no debt at that time, except for a car payment. This information agreed with the credit check. The written references that they had given me seemed authentic and because I obtained a positive credit check on them, I never contacted any of the people that wrote them. But I was going to call them now.

The phone number for the first reference was out of service. A lady picked up when I dialed the second number and said Wellness Drugs. I asked for Caroline Westly and was told that she hadn't worked there in over two years. I asked her if she had a phone number or a forwarding address for Caroline and, surprisingly, the lady gave me her address. She had no phone number for Caroline but she had heard that she was working at a diner on South Canal Street and had married some guy named Brown.

I did my homework and, thanks to the internet, I learned that they were deep in debt. They had a mortgage on the diner and the home that they had just purchased a couple of months ago. They also drove two leased vehicles. The four other people that I had seen coming and going were their kids. They had two bank accounts at the River Heights Bank, one business and one personal. In addition, their address was the same as the one I had been given for Caroline Westly-Brown.

I found the number for the B and L Diner on the internet and called, only to get a message that they were closed for the day. It was Sunday.

After dinner, I decided to drive by the Brown house and check out the activity. I knew where they worked and I knew where they lived. My best guess was that at least six people were living in that small house. The biggest problem I was having was trying to figure out the delivery system for the poison. Perhaps, I should just burn their damn house down while they were all asleep. It would be fast and simple and I'd probably be seen sneaking around the house by some nosey neighbor and wind up being fried in the electric chair.

The street where the Browns lived was busy. The weather was getting warmer and there were a lot of people outside, some shopping and some just sitting on their front stairs and visiting. For the first time since I had started watching the Brown's house, I saw a couple of gangs of teenage boys standing around looking like they were up to no good.

It was clear that I had to be far away and have one good alibi when they died.

My time was up. Dr. Miller and I said our goodbyes and I stopped by the receptionist's desk as I was leaving. She handed me a bill and I told her I would bring a check with me tomorrow.

Fourteen

I took a long weekend and flew to Charleston to spend Easter with my parents. The non-stop flight took just a little over two hours and I spent most of that time thinking about the Browns. I still hadn't come up with a failsafe plan and it was driving me nuts.

I had stopped driving by their house a few weeks ago. No point in calling attention to myself. I still occasionally parked outside the diner and watched Missy and Rodney. It seemed their routine never varied. Missy always went to the bank right before she left work to go home. The only day she didn't go straight home was on Thursday when she stopped by Wholesome Foods and did her grocery shopping. Rodney always closed up the diner and went straight home. The help, which was all family, came and went during the day and I could never keep their hours straight, as there was no pattern as to who worked when.

I had only met the Browns once when I interviewed them before I rented my apartment to them. I wondered if they would still recognize me if they saw me now. I decided to chance it. I left work early on a Thursday and followed Missy to the grocery store. As she shopped, I walked behind her, staying close enough so that I could see what she put into her cart but far enough away so that I didn't bring attention to myself.

She bought a few staples, along with some frozen dinners and fast-food items. Mostly, though, it was junk food she went for, including six frozen pizzas, cookies, cakes, and candy. Obviously, she did most of her cooking at the diner and not a lot at home. She stopped in the coffee aisle and used the store grinder to grind up a couple of pounds of the French Roast coffee. While she was in the liquor department of the store Missy picked up a couple of twelve-packs of pop, a twelve-pack of beer, and six bottles of wine.

Now, flying into Charleston, a plan started to form. If it worked, I would be golden. If not, well - we'd see.

I had been around Dr. Miller long enough to know when he was about to interrupt me. He got this puzzling look on his face that looked like he was wondering if he should talk or keep quiet. Usually, the talking won out, as it did now. "Sydney, tell me. When you got back from Ireland and found your apartment trashed, why didn't you call the police? They owed you rent for the three months they didn't pay and the damage to your place was horrific. Couldn't you have had them arrested? The least you could have done is sued for damages to get reimbursed."

"It never crossed my mind to call the police. This was my problem and I needed to fix it. Yes, it was a lot of money, but recouping it wouldn't mean anything. I needed to get even. Going through the legal system wouldn't give me the satisfaction—the feeling. I needed the feeling I get of knowing that someone has paid. Do you really think I was going to get that from waiting years for the legal system to do its job? And, then they'd cry that they didn't have any money. It would be like trying to get blood out of a turnip. And, they'd still be around laughing about it. No one laughs at me and gets away with it, Doctor. No one."

"So, you finally had a plan. Tell me about it," Dr. Miller said, changing the subject back to what I had been talking about in the first place.

I flew into Charleston on Saturday afternoon, planning to fly back to Chicago on Monday. I had a wonderful Easter with my family. My sister and her family were there and we caught up on our lives. My mom did the whole Easter dinner thing and I ate like a pig.

My dad, who was diabetic, had to have insulin injections on a daily basis and kept his hypodermic needles in the kitchen cupboard. While I was there, I took one and I put it in the side pocket of my suitcase. I would only need one.

As soon as we landed back in Chicago, I exited the plane, retrieved my car from the lot where it was parked, and headed straight for a liquor store. Once there I purchased two bottles each of the finest Riesling, muscatel, and chardonnay wine that I could find.

I was anxious to see if my plan would work but I was just as tired as excited when I finally got home. Tired won out and I decided to call it a night and hit the hay. The next day was going to be extremely busy at work and I needed to be at my best. Mr. Lilly and Mr. Little had called a meeting to discuss the feasibility of opening a branch office in Copenhagen. All board members were to be present. I had to be alert and at my best.

The next day dragged by. The meeting took longer than expected and I left work after seven, worn out. On my way home, I ordered a pizza to be delivered and figured it would probably reach my apartment about the same time I did.

I had no more than taken off my jacket when the doorbell rang. It was the delivery boy with my pizza. I ate about half of it, put the rest in the fridge, and got to work.

I carefully removed the powder from one of the capsules and put it into a small deep bowl. Using sterile water and adding a few drops at a time the mixture eventually went from paste to liquid. The next step was to fill the syringe and inject the solution through the corks into the bottles. It wouldn't take much and I didn't think I had to worry about any sediment showing up at the bottom of the bottles.

I opened my suitcase, which was still in my bedroom, and unpacked. I took out the syringe. I took it out of its wrapping and looked at it, I started to swear. I was fucked. It was only a 6mm needle and there was no way it was going to fit through the cork so I could insert the solution into the wine. I needed a longer needle and I wasn't even sure if they made them long enough to fit through a cork.

"I did not see that coming," said Dr. Miller. "I can imagine you were extremely upset after going through all that only to have your plan blow up because of the size of a needle."

"If that was today it wouldn't have been a problem. Now you can even buy syringes and needles on Amazon," I replied.

So, what did you decide to do next? Did you ever accomplish your goal, Sydney?"

"Do you remember any headlines from the summer of 1993?"

"1993? That was a long time ago."

"Family Found Dead in Chicago Home--Baby Only Survivor"

"Oh, my God! That was you?"

"We have run way over my hour, Doc. See you Monday. Have a good weekend," I replied, ignoring the look of shock on his face. This was the best moment I'd had in the past three weeks. For a few seconds, that glorious feeling came over me – the feeling that made me whole and alive.

But, just for a few seconds.

Fifteen

It's Saturday morning and I'm sitting at my kitchen table, drinking a cup of coffee and looking at the bill from Dr. Miller. I had ten visits over a period of three weeks. I'm a little surprised at the total cost to date, as I expected the bill to be more. He had only charged me for an hour for each visit, even though some have gone way over that time. I certainly have no complaints and I make a mental note to be sure to pay him on Monday.

So far, my memory is okay. My headaches have been greatly reduced in intensity due to the new medication I'm taking. I have noticed that my balance is a little shaky at times but nothing to be too concerned about. Dr. Fuller told me what signs to look for and what I can expect. My six months to live is now five or less.

Mr. Lilly is gone now and Mr. Little has just turned the reins over to his son. I wonder how many people go through life only having one job. It's hard to believe that it's been eight years already since I retired. For thirty years, my job had been my life. It would have been so different if Quinn had lived. We would have had a family and maybe I would have been a grandparent by now. The only person I ever cared about has been gone twenty-two years now and I'm still mourning my loss.

I look out the kitchen window and watch a yellow

finch at the birdbath. My backyard is private and backs up to a wooded area. Living in the country means I always have some type of wildlife around to entertain me.

I have an appointment with Dr. Fuller this morning. It seems that all I do these days is go to doctors' appointments.

As I leave my house and pull out of the driveway, I notice a black van parked a little way down the road. I don't recognize it as being one of the neighbors' cars and decide to check it out. So, instead of turning right, I make a left and as I approach the vehicle, I see two bodies slouching down in their seats. I glance at the license plate as I continue past the van and make a mental note to check it out later.

I'm not even half a mile down the road before it hits me. That was the same van that cut me off that day in the parking lot.

Is it possible that, after my stupid visit to the FBI three weeks ago, they have identified me and are watching me? I'm sure I showed up on some security cameras entering and exiting the building, but I would have to be in a facial recognition program for them to ID me. Or, would I? Perhaps just running it against the Bureau of Motor Vehicles would do the trick.

Something was going on and I had no idea what.

Sixteen

I stood in the kitchen and looked at the syringe. I needed to get my wits about me. What the hell was I doing? I'd been running around like an idiot, coming up with wild ideas that didn't work and not thinking anything through. It was time to step back and start thinking with a cool head. Revenge would come, but it didn't have to come today or tomorrow. After all, it took me ten years to give Tony and Pat their payback. And, it was sweet. That's what I wanted now. The same sweet revenge with that glorious feeling that followed.

For the next three weeks, I left work at two-thirty on Thursdays. I would go to the grocery store and wait for Missy Brown to show up to do her shopping. Each time I followed behind her and watched her shop she never varied in her routine. She bought the same type of items that she had purchased the first time I followed her. Each week she filled her cart with pizzas and junk food, some staples, ground coffee, and the same six bottles of wine.

I decided that three weeks gave me enough information about her shopping habits and that I would take action on the fourth week. I left work at two that following Thursday instead of two-thirty. I drove to the Wholesome Foods Grocery Store and started shopping. When I reached the coffee aisle, I ground up two pounds of the same coffee that Missy bought every week. I opened a capsule and sprinkled the powder on the ground coffee, gave the bag a little shake to mix it up, and closed it.

Missy arrived right on schedule. I slowly pushed my cart behind her as she proceeded to fill her cart with all the same crap she bought week after week. I waited until she had ground her coffee and put it into her cart before I made my move. As I started to go by her, I knocked a couple of containers of Ned's Coffee Creamer off the shelf and they fell behind her onto the floor. She swung around, startled by the noise, and, as I continued by her, I grabbed her coffee out of her cart and replaced it with mine. I have to say, the transfer went as smooth as any magician's trick. Fortunately, no one was watching.

I headed for the pharmacy department to pick up a few items and waited. Once Missy had checked out and was gone, I paid for my items, left the store, and drove home.

Now it was just a matter of waiting and watching the news.

"Seven people died, Sydney," Dr. Miller interrupted. "You poisoned that entire family. You made a baby an orphan. The story was in the papers for days. People were in an uproar demanding justice. That family lay dead in that house for two days before they were found. That baby was found crawling around on the floor, dirty and hungry."

"They ruined my apartment. It wasn't just Rodney and Missy that did it. It was their whole rotten family. I never expected that seven people would die, though. I still haven't figured out how they all died at the same time. Did they all sit down and have coffee together? Maybe that was their morning routine. Plan out the work schedule for the day? You know, like who's working and when. They were found in different rooms. It's too bad about the baby. I didn't know about her. But, again, Doc, that's the price of doing business. And, by the way, it was eight not seven."

"No. I definitely recall that seven people were found dead," Dr. Miller said.

"Seven were found that day," I said. "However, Missy had a sister who lived in Carbondale. They weren't close, as she was quite a bit older than Missy was. Her name was Caroline Simpson and she was the only surviving relative of Missy. Rodney's family was gone. Never knew his parents and his two brothers were killed in a drive-by shooting years ago. A couple of weeks after the police released the crime scene Caroline hired a company to come in and clean up the house. She intended to put it up for sale and wanted to get it on the market as soon as possible. Once the cleaners finished up, she had an estate sale, and what didn't sell she gave to some charity. Everything in the refrigerator had either been tossed out or taken to the police lab for testing. But, for some reason, they left the stuff that was stored in the kitchen cabinets, which included the bag of coffee. Caroline couldn't bring herself to toss out almost two pounds of good coffee, so she put the bag of coffee in a box with some other items and took it home."

"And, she made coffee with it and died," Dr. Miller said with a sigh.

"That's what happened. The thing is, she used up her coffee before she opened the bag she took from her sister's house. Her death happened about four weeks later. The coroner said heart attack and that was that. They never connected her death with the deaths of the Browns family."

"They never did find out what killed the Browns, did they?" Dr. Miller asked.

"Inconclusive. Oh, the police figured they had been poisoned, they just didn't know how. They ran every test available and checked for every possible poison. The thing is, Doc, is that there is no test for the Doll's Eyes toxin. It's never been developed and the toxin is undetectable. A few kids die every year from eating the berry. The authorities know because death is immediate and they always find the bodies near the plant. It doesn't take a rocket scientist to figure out that they died from eating the berries."

"So, one more death was again just the price of doing business, Sydney?"

"How was I to know the greedy bitch would take the coffee home? I don't consider that one my fault at all," I replied.

"Tell me how you felt after you found out that your plan had worked. Did you feel the same amount of satisfaction that you felt when you killed Tony and Pat?"

"It was even better," I replied. "So much better."

"So that's it then. These are the people you want me to tell the FBI about after you pass away. That's quite a list, Sydney."

"Oh, no, Doc. We're not done yet," I replied.

Seventeen

For about a week after the Browns died, I was on such a high that people at work asked me if I was okay. I was so happy that I had to concentrate on not smiling all the time. Then, out of nowhere, the depression hit.

The first day I just thought I was having a bad day and tried to shake it off. By the third day, I was having trouble getting out of bed and now people at work were again asking me if I was okay, but for a different reason.

I decided that I was feeling the after-effects of losing Quinn. I had been so busy with my obsession with the Browns that I never properly mourned my loss. Now that my mind wasn't fixated on the Browns, Quinn was all I could think about. I was sinking deeper and deeper into a pit and I couldn't think of one reason why I should even try to get out.

On the fourth day, Mr. Lilly called me into his office for a chat. He asked me what was wrong and if there was some way he could help. We discussed how I was feeling and why and it was decided that I should take some time off work and get some help. He said he would call me later with the name of a good therapist who might be able to help me through this difficult time.

It took me six months before I was well enough to go back to work. I saw the therapist Mr. Lilly recommended and it helped. We only discussed Quinn. He felt that was the root cause of what I was going through and that was what we needed to address. He helped me understand that I didn't have to forget Quinn and I could always cherish the time we shared. I should not feel guilty for what happened and the fact that I was still alive. It wasn't my fault and I needed to get on with my life.

During the time I was off work, Mr. Lilly temporarily promoted Jason Summerfield to fill my position. He was good at the job and it was obvious he wasn't too happy when I made my return appearance. The staff had a cake and a card that was signed by everyone welcoming me back. Jason stayed in the background and simply glared at me.

For the first few weeks after I was back, people pretty much treated me with kid's gloves. They were quiet and watched how they phrased things around me. There was very little joking when they were around me. I decided to break the ice and showed up at work one morning wearing a pair of Groucho Marx glasses. That did the trick and things slowly settled back into normal.

"I assume you were on anti-depressants during this time. Are you still on them?" Dr. Miller inquired.

"That's the thing. I was told I would probably need them for the rest of my life. I stopped taking them a few days after I went back to work. They made me hazy feeling and tired. My job demanded that I be alert and at my best. So, I quit taking them."

"Did you ever struggle with depression again? It seems very strange that you would have one bout and be over it forever."

"Never to the degree that I didn't want to get out of bed. Even now, knowing I am dying, I'm not depressed. Although, I've been told that's a symptom and it still may happen," I replied.

"Yes, a brain tumor can cause mood swings among many other things. I've been meaning to ask you, Sydney, if you are still getting bad headaches?"

"Not so much. The new medication that Dr. Fuller has me on works well most of the time. The headaches seem to be under control for now."

Things went well for the next couple of years. Except for a few fast trips to Copenhagen, where we had finally opened a branch office, and to check out Tokyo as a possible new location, I pretty much stayed in Chicago.

I watched Jason move up the corporate ladder and it was obvious he was shooting for my job. Mr. Lilly seemed to have taken a real liking to him. This became even more obvious when he announced that Jason would be traveling to Tokyo to help start up a branch office there. The fact that he would be out of the office for a few years was gratifying but his new position in the company was unsettling. Jason had only been with the company for five years. I needed to keep an eye on him. He was moving too fast.

"So, is Jason the next one I'm adding to my list for the FBI?" Dr. Miller asked.

"You're getting impatient, Doctor. You know I never jump ahead in a story. Time to go, isn't it?"

"Yes, Sydney, time's up," he replied and sighed.

Eighteen

I needed to pick up a refill of my headache medicine, so when I left Dr. Miller's office I headed for the drugstore. As I pull into the parking lot, I notice a black van slowly drive by the entrance to the store and continue on down the street. There was little doubt in my mind that the FBI was keeping an eye on me. I just didn't know for what reason.

The fact that they were still following me was unsettling. I figured they would have approached me by now if this was about that visit I had made to their offices weeks ago. After all, I had walked into their building and said I had information about some murders.

When I left the store, they were parked across the street. Either they didn't care that I saw them or they needed to take a class on how to tail someone.

I pulled out of the parking lot into the street and watched in my rear-view mirror as they pulled in behind me.

I made a left at the next corner and then made a right. I continued to zigzag from one street to another, all the while watching them follow me. Finally, I said to hell with it. Obviously, they knew that I knew they were tailing me and they weren't even trying to hide it. I drove home, wondering what the fuck was going on and what I was going to do about it.

Nineteen

There was an unwritten company policy that executive employees had to open two branch offices before being promoted to a top-level position. In some cases, this meant that you could be out of the States for two or three years at a time. I loved setting up offices in other countries. However, this 'policy' was a real hardship to some of my fellow employees, especially those with families. Over the years I watched quite a few of them leave the company for less stressful positions.

I saw Jason a few times over the next two years. He traveled back to Chicago about every six months to update Mr. Lilly and Mr. Little on the progress of the Tokyo office. The startup had been slow going, but business had picked up and it looked like the decision to open a branch office there was going to pay off.

You would have thought Jason was a hero returning from the war when the Tokyo office was ready to operate on its own and he returned home to stay. Mr. Lilly and Mr. Little announced that Jason had been promoted to General Manager. A private office on the tenth floor was being renovated for him. Jason would start his new position in a couple of weeks. Until then, he would be taking some personal time off.

What the fuck was going on? I was Deputy General

Manager and now this little snot-nosed kid was promoted to a position higher than mine. He hadn't paid his dues like the rest of us. I wasn't the only one pissed off in the office that day and the water cooler seemed to be the most popular spot in the office. It was while I was passing the water cooler that I heard one of my fellow employees use the word nepotism.

I turned around and looked at the five people standing there talking and asked if I had heard right. I was told that Jason was Mr. Lilly's nephew. How did I not know this? This wasn't right, nephew or not. Jason wasn't about to take the position that was rightfully mine.

It had been sixteen years since I had made my Doll's Eyes powder. It had been about five years since I had last used it. I had no idea if it was ever going to lose its potency, but I knew I was about to find out.

Jason was not a good-looking man. He was probably only five foot, seven inches, had premature balding, and was extremely overweight. He was not married and lived alone. Other than this information, I knew very little about his day-to-day lifestyle or his likes and dislikes. It was time to find out.

The following day I knocked on Mr. Lilly's office door and asked if he had a minute. Like always, he stopped what he was doing and welcomed me in. I mentioned that some of us at work were talking about taking Jason out for a welcome-home dinner and wondered if he knew what his favorite foods were. Mr. Lilly beamed as he told me that the idea was extremely considerate and he was pleased that we were taking the time and effort to welcome Jason back. It seemed that there was nothing that Jason didn't eat, although he was not particularly fond of Chinese or Japanese foods. I bit my tongue when I heard that, as he had just spent two years living in Japan and I wondered what he ate while he was there. Although, by the way he looked, I was sure he had made many trips to McDonald's.

After leaving Mr. Lilly's office, I asked around to see if any of my co-workers were up for the idea. There were no takers. No one wanted to go to dinner with Jason.

I thought about my options. I could ask Jason to dinner but it would just be the two of us. I could give him a big box of chocolates or a fruit basket to welcome his arrival back at work. Then the possibility existed that he might share and others would die. Or, I could just shoot the fat bastard.

I thought about how long it took for Pat and Tony to die. I had not added very much powder to their drinks and it took a couple of hours for them to die. A little less powder meant it would take a little longer to work and with Jason's size, it would probably extend the time even more.

Dinner would be a nice way to go, I decided.

I went back to my office, looked up Jason's cell phone number, and called him. He answered on the first ring and seemed shocked but excited when I asked him to dinner the following Friday night.

We had a nice dinner and talked about his new position with the company. He was excited but also nervous about it and he hoped he wouldn't disappoint his uncle. He didn't want coffee after dinner but decided a brandy would be nice to finish off his meal. He excused himself to use the washroom and I simply added a very small amount of the Doll's Eye powder to his drink.

The next morning the local news reported that Jason's body had been found in an alley behind a bar in Boy's Town. He died somewhere between twelve and one. A blood test showed that he had an alcohol blood level of 1.6 when he died. The coroner ruled his death due to heart failure.

At the time of his death, I was home in bed sound asleep.

"How do you think Jason's promotion would have affected you and your job? Were you concerned about being let go?" Dr. Miller asked me.

"First of all, he hadn't earned his bones. One new opening in one city wasn't the rule. Everyone but him had to pay the price. Not the boss' nephew. Well, it wasn't fair. I didn't like him. Nobody did. I did the world a favor by getting rid of him. I should have been thanked," I replied. "And no, I wasn't concerned about being let go. Jason was given the position that was to be my next step up the ladder. I had no place to move up with Jason being put into that position."

"Did you ever move up in the company?"

"Oh, I moved up alright. I had Jason's position within two weeks of his death."

"I don't get it," Doctor Miller said. "Why would your boss promote you so soon after Jason's death?"

"Because, I was the only one who went to dinner with Jason."

Twenty

Driving home from my session with Dr. Miller I thought back on my life and how hard it was to believe that it was ending. Dr. Fuller had suggested that if there was anything still undone on my bucket list I should get with it, as time was running out. The funny thing is that since I started taking the headache medicine, I'm feeling better than I had felt a month ago. It was hard to comprehend that in a few months I wouldn't be here.

I couldn't think of one thing I still wanted to do. I had my affairs in order. My sister didn't need the money, so we decided that everything would go to her daughter, Alexa, and my brother's son, Jon. They would split my estate, which would make them both wealthy. My home in Munster, which I had brought after I retired, was worth well over a million alone. That, with all my investments, savings, and retirement plans would make them both set for life.

Then I saw the black van following me and I got pissed. I was tired of this bull crap. Perhaps I should add something to my bucket list.

I was just about ready to turn to take the road to my house when I decided to take a drive. I turned my car around in a stranger's driveway and headed back the way I had come. My first stop was at a car wash. The line was fairly long, so it took quite a while before I entered the car wash. I ordered the deluxe service, got out of my car, and walked into the main office to pay. I glanced out the window and saw the van sitting by the exit, waiting.

After I retrieved my nice clean car, I drove to Culvers. I ordered a burger and a shake. I took my time eating, while the guys in the van sat in the parking lot and waited.

Then I drove down Indianapolis St. and made a left turn, which took me to a local theater. I parked my car, went in, bought a ticket, and spent the next hour in the theater watching the first part of a bad movie. As I got up to exit the theater, I saw Frick and Frack sitting in the back of the theater. They were so absorbed in the movie they never saw me leave. As soon as I was in the parking lot, I walked over to their car, and, using my car key, I left a scratch the entire length of their vehicle. Childish? Yes. But it made me feel good.

For the first time in a couple of weeks, I drove home without being followed.

I decided to buy a gun.

Twenty-One

We were in the middle of a session when I suddenly changed the subject.

"I've decided to buy a gun," I told Dr. Miller. "I should have bought one a long time ago. I live on the edge of town. In the country really. If I need help or if I'm in danger, it would take the police a long time to get to my house. I think I would feel safer if I had a gun."

"What makes you think you are going to be in danger? Did something happen?" Dr. Miller asked.

"I'm being followed."

"Sydney, I doubt very much that you are being followed. Why would anyone want to follow you? I'm sure you don't have anything to worry about. At this point it would just be a waste of money, don't you think? You're just being paranoid."

"Perhaps so, but I think I would feel safer. It would put my mind to rest knowing I could protect myself. You live around here, doctor. Do you know a place that sells guns? And, a shooting range. I will need to practice shooting. Do you know where there is a shooting range?" I asked.

"It's really a bad idea, Sydney, for you to have a gun. You should think about this before you do anything rash. I'm sure this is just your imagination."

"You think so? I don't think my buying a gun is rash.

Lots of people have guns. And, Doctor, I'm positive I'm being followed."

"Sydney, are you planning on doing bodily harm to someone?"

I gave a half laugh as I answered, "Why would you ask me that question? Of course not. I just think I'd feel better with a gun."

"I'm afraid it's out of the question. You definitely should not buy a gun," he replied.

"Well, maybe I will or maybe I won't. We'll see."

Obviously, this conversation was making Dr. Miller extremely uncomfortable. I wasn't sure if it was because he was afraid I'd shoot him or if it was because he knew I was being followed. Something about the way he was acting wasn't right. He might have said something to the FBI about me being dangerous. He couldn't divulge what I told him during our sessions, but if he said he was afraid I might do something, they would probably watch me.

Right now, there was no doubt in my mind that Dr. Miller was afraid of me. And, he should be. If I found out that he had talked to the FBI, he would be dead long before my time was up.

"Should we get back on track and continue?" he asked. "Your hour isn't up yet."

A year had passed since I had killed Jason. My

promotion came with a lot more responsibility than what I had in my previous position. Once again, I started doing a lot of traveling. One aspect of my job was to troubleshoot our branch offices. If an office didn't meet its quota or if it had some internal problems, I was the one who was called on to fix it.

Mr. Lilly had received a call from Charles, the manager of our London office. He told Mr. Lilly that someone had robbed the office and set a fire to try to cover it up. Mr. Lilly informed him that he would be sending someone to London immediately to address this situation.

Mr. Lilly then called me into his office and told me that I needed to get to London as soon as possible. I had my assistant make my reservations for travel and headed home to pack.

As soon as I arrived in London, I checked into the Dorchester Hotel, where I would be staying. I dropped off my bags and headed to our office. Once there, I met with Charles, who told me that we were extremely lucky that the fire had mostly been confined to Charles' office. The rest of the offices had sustained little damage. There had been some smoke damage, but cleaners had already been in and taken care of that. Charles' office, however, would have to be completely restored.

Seven employees were working in the London office. Besides Charles, there were three other consultants, two administrative assistants, and Pete, who they called Gopher. Pete did all sorts of odd jobs around the office, including stocking, shopping, cleaning, filing, and whatever else was necessary. I interviewed all of them and they all told me they liked their jobs and had no grudges or problems with Charles or the company.

I made an appointment with the Fire Investigation Unit Chief who had investigated the fire. He met me at the office the next day and he told me that an accelerant had definitely been used to start the fire. The only reason that the entire building didn't burn down was because of the excellent alarm and sprinkling systems that had been installed. It had only taken the fire trucks minutes to arrive after the alarms went off.

After my discussion with the Fire Chief was over, I asked Charles to drive me to the police station. I wanted to talk to the detective in charge of this case. She basically repeated what Charles had told me, which was that the fire had been started to cover up the robbery. They found no signs of a break-in and whoever set the fire probably had access to the building. There was no question that the security cameras had been disabled. She said they were still checking the neighborhood to see if other cameras in the area picked up any activity at the time of the fire.

There wasn't much more that I could do. The investigation was in good hands and both the Fire Chief and the Police Detective assured me that they would keep me informed if they had any new news.

I called Mr. Lilly and told him of my findings. For the first time since I had known him, I heard Mr. Lilly swear. He told me not to come home until the fucking bastard had been caught and punished. He apologized to me for his language and hung up.

I seem to remember it took a long time before my jaw was back where it belonged.

"This was out of character for Mr. Lilly? The swearing, I mean," Dr. Miller said.

"Are you kidding? I believe I mentioned that if any of us got a little raunchy or off-color, we would be called into his office and given a lecture. We signed contracts with moral clauses. For him to swear? Well, let's say that I expected the world to end right there and then."

"Did you ever find the person who started it?" Dr. Miller asked me.

"Actually, the police did. It was Pete."

"Pete, the gopher?"

"Yes, Pete the gopher," I answered.

"I assume that Pete is dead," Dr. Miller said.

"No. Pete is alive and in prison," I said.

"Oh. I thought there was going to be more to this story. I guess that's it for today, Sydney. By the way, tomorrow makes it four weeks since you've been seeing me. Do you have any idea how many more visits before we wrap this up?"

"I don't know. Probably a few more, possibly a week. I figure we should be done by the end of next week."

"See you tomorrow, Sydney. And, don't buy a gun."

"Tomorrow, Doc," I replied.

Twenty-Two

I had no plans to do anything after I left Dr. Miller's office so I headed home. I watched the black van pull in behind me keeping its usual distance between us. After driving about half a mile, the van suddenly did a uey in the middle of the road and headed in the opposite direction. I caught myself breathing a sigh of relief. I guess being followed was bothering me a lot more than I cared to admit.

After an uneventful night, I woke up with a pounding headache. I had forgotten to take my medication and I was paying for it now. I took a pill with my first cup of coffee and waited for it to kick in. Finally, after about fifteen minutes, I started to get some relief. I checked the time and decided to get showered and dressed. I had some yard work to do this morning and decided to hold off on the shower until after I finished up outside. I would be hot and sweaty when I finished in the yard and it didn't make sense to take two showers.

The next thing I knew forty-five minutes had passed and I was still sitting at the table. I had no memory of time passing. I sat there wondering what had happened. Then my heart started pounding as I realized I had just had a seizure. I had experienced a loss of awareness. I guessed that it was a petit mal seizure.

I debated calling the doctor and telling her what had

happened. I was pretty sure that she would tell me to quit driving, and I wasn't ready to do that. I decided to risk it and not say anything.

The second seizure hit me as I was walking to the bedroom. My leg muscles stiffened up and I fell to the floor. Then my arms started to twitch. The whole episode only lasted less than a minute. I stayed on the floor and took deep breaths, slowly returning to normal. When I felt it was safe, I stood up and fell onto my bed.

I spent the better part of the morning dozing off and on. Finally, around noon, I got up, showered, and got dressed. To hell with the weeds. They would still be there tomorrow.

Twenty-three

I had been in London for three weeks and was planning to leave to go back to the States in a few days. A contractor had been hired who repaired the damage done to the offices. By the end of the third week, everything was looking good and business was back to normal. The investigation into the robbery and fire had been closed and Pete was sitting in jail waiting to be sentenced. He had pled guilty so there was no need for a trial.

Charles and I had developed a good friendship while I was there and on numerous occasions, he had me over to his home for dinner. His wife, Beth, was a great cook, and having a home-cooked meal once in a while was a real treat.

A few days before I was to leave to go back to Chicago, Charles and Beth invited me over for a farewell meal. I had heard on numerous occasions about Beth's 'famous Shepherd's Pie,' and she was making it for dinner.

It was a nice evening. We had a couple of drinks before we ate and I enjoyed a fantastic meal. The Shepherd's Pie was all that it was cracked up to be. I said my farewell to Beth and left with Charles, who drove me back to my hotel.

When we pulled up in front of the hotel Charles asked me if he could come up to my room for a few minutes. There was something he wanted to discuss with me in private, and he didn't know if he would get the chance at the office. I said fine and I would wait for him in the lobby while he parked the car. He was back in a few minutes and we entered the elevator to go to my room. As the elevator started to ascend, Charles suddenly pushed me back up against the wall and tried to kiss me. He muttered some nonsense about how he knew I wanted him as bad as he wanted me. He pinned my arms with one hand while trying to undo my pants with the other. As I tried to push him away, he spun me around and knocked my head hard into the wall, leaving me slightly dazed. Before I knew what happened he had pulled my pants down.

He reached over and hit the stop button on the elevator. As I tried to turn around, he hit me hard in the face and told me to get on my knees. I tried to push away from him but he hit me for a second time and I was down. I was almost unconscious but I'll never forget the sound of him unzipping his pants. Then he rolled me over onto my stomach and sodomized me, all the while telling me he knew how much I loved it.

It probably took less than a minute. He got off me, hit the stop button, and the elevator continued to my floor. He helped me up and held my arm until the elevator stopped and the door opened. The fucker actually thanked me for a nice evening and then practically shoved me out the door. He hit the down button, the door closed and he was gone.

"He raped you? My god, that's terrible. What did you do?" Dr. Miller interrupted.

"I got on a plane the next day and flew back to Chicago. I went to my house, got some powder, and flew right back to London. No one even knew I made the trip," I replied.

"You killed him. Right?"

"Damn right, I did. And, I watched him die."

Two days later, I walked into the office in London with a small bottle of Dewar's Scotch whiskey tucked away in my briefcase. Charles greeted me as if nothing had happened and asked where I had been for the past couple of days. I told him I was leaving and needed to talk to him privately in his office.

We went into his office and I shut the door. He smiled a creepy leering smile, winked at me, and said he was going to miss me. I reached into my briefcase, took out the bottle of scotch, and asked if he would like a farewell drink.

I poured two drinks. Charles had his drink gone before I even started to pick my glass up. I refilled his glass and, as he picked it up to drink, I told him that I hoped he rotted in hell.

I watched him die. Just like Elsie had done, he grabbed at his chest, gave me a blank stare, and died. I turned his chair around so he wasn't facing the door, put the bottle back in my briefcase, and walked to the washroom with the two glasses. I dumped the scotch that was still in my glass out in the sink. Then I washed both of the glasses and put them in my jacket pocket.

I went back to Charles' office, wiped my fingerprints off the glasses, and put them back on the shelf. Making sure his office door was shut, I went out to the reception area, said a fast goodbye to everyone who was there, and left. I was on a flight back to Chicago two hours later, which was just about the same time that someone found Charles slumped down in his chair.

"Once again, you handed out your own justice," Dr. Miller said. "So, what did they say happened to Charles? Surely, there was an investigation into his death."

"Once again," I mimicked him, "The cause of death was heart failure. So sad for such a young man, everyone said. His wife was devastated, of course. I found out later that she was pregnant. I figure I did her a favor. He was a rapist. Who knows how many others there were besides me?"

"It had to be terrible for you. I'm so sorry, Sydney, that you had to go through that. I have to admit, though, that I figured it would be Pete you would do in."

"What Pete did wasn't a personal affront to me. He did it to the company. He was punished exactly the way he should have been. Charles? He got off way too easy. I wished he had suffered more. His death didn't give me the satisfaction that I got from the others. I needed more and I walked away empty."

"You still think you are being followed?" Dr. Miller asked, changing the subject.

"You know, that's the funniest thing. I was positive I was being followed when I left here yesterday. Now I'm not sure. Maybe it is just my imagination."

"Of course, it is. Why would anyone want to follow you? You need to relax, Sydney."

"Or, it could be that they were told to back off," I said.

"Is there anything else you want to discuss before we call it a day?"

"I guess that's it. We have a long weekend, so I guess I won't see you until Tuesday."

"Yes, Tuesday it is. Have a good weekend," Dr. Miller replied.

I stood and looked at him. He was flushed and he looked away. Oh, Doctor, I thought, what have you been up to?

Twenty-four

I sat in my car thinking about what had just happened. In Indiana, you can walk into a gun store, buy a gun, and walk out five minutes later as a gun owner. I had just been refused the purchase of a handgun and had been told that my request to buy a gun was put into a 'delayed' status. It could take up to three days before the owner of the store was contacted with a yes or no answer regarding my purchasing a handgun.

Normally all it took was a valid driver's license and a five-minute background check and you were good to go. I had no criminal background and had never so much as had a traffic ticket. So why was I being treated like a criminal? It had to be the fucking FBI messing with me.

I couldn't prove it but I was pretty sure Dr. Miller had contacted the feds shortly after I started seeing him. Perhaps he was afraid I was going to do something violent. Perhaps he was just covering all his bases in case something happened to him. Whatever was going on, I was on some type of a list.

I started my car and drove off. It was the first day of a three-day weekend and traffic was heavy. I had some shopping that should be done but decided it could wait a few days. I didn't feel like fighting the crowds. Plus, I needed to cut the grass and do some weeding, so I decided I would just go home and take care of that.

The next thing I knew someone was pounding on my car window asking me if I was okay. I glanced up and realized that I was in the middle of the street blocking traffic. I had just experienced another seizure.

I rolled down my window and told the man I was okay and apologized. I pulled my car into a parking spot and sat there. The one thing I was concerned about had happened. I had a seizure while driving. This time I lucked out but what if it happened again?

I made it home without any other incidents and spent most of the afternoon working in my yard. I loved my house and had spent the last seven years of my retirement there. After I retired and sold my apartment, I wondered if buying a home was the right thing to do. Now, as I sat on the patio and watched the birds fight over the bird food, a deep sadness came over me. I didn't want to leave this. I didn't want to die. I knew the worst was yet to come. The doctor had said maybe six months. So, if I was lucky, I had a little over four to go.

My memory wasn't as good as it used to be, but still not bad. I had experienced three seizures, but none of them were extreme. The headaches persisted but were not nearly as bad as before I started on the new medication. All in all, I was doing pretty well.

There was no way of knowing if the seizures would

increase in intensity. There was also no way of knowing if or when I would get any of the other symptoms that came with this rotten disease. Just the luck of the draw, I guess. I just hoped I was dead before I totally lost it.

I started wondering again why I had been refused the gun. I hadn't thought too much about the feds since I stopped seeing the black van. The day it turned around and quit following me was the last time I had seen it. That was the same day I had mentioned that I thought I was being followed to Dr. Miller. Did he call and tell them to back off? I trusted him less and less.

Perhaps I should start paying more attention to the traffic around me. Just because I didn't see that black van didn't mean the feds weren't still watching me.

Twenty-five

On Sunday, I played a game. I got in my car and went for ten or fifteen-minute drives. I drove to the gas station and filled up my car with gas. Then I drove home. An hour later I went to the grocery store, bought a loaf of bread, and drove home. Two hours after that, I dropped some clothes off at the dry cleaners. This continued for the rest of the day and part of Monday.

It was probably childish, but it accomplished its purpose. Each time I left the house, I saw a silver sedan following me. The car kept quite a distance between us but it was obvious that the feds were still in the picture. I was not going to let on that I knew I was being followed. This time I was going to let nature take its course.

On Tuesday afternoon, I was back in Dr. Miller's office for my usual session. He was very talkative, which was unusual for him.

"Did you enjoy your weekend, Sydney? Did you do anything special? I had a very nice time with my family. Saturday, I took the kids to Six Flags, which is always a great time for them. I'm getting a little too old for some of those rides, but I did try out a few new ones. Then we had a cookout with a bunch of the neighbors on Sunday. Ate way too much. Monday I just stayed at home. I did a little yard work, but mostly just relaxed. I feel totally refreshed today. I guess I needed a few days off to unwind. So, how about you? What did you do?"

"Sounds like you had a nice full weekend," I replied. "I didn't do much. I did some yard work, too. That's a non-ending job. Mostly I just rested."

"Well, resting is good. You probably need more rest now. How are you feeling?" Dr. Miller asked.

"I feel great, considering I have less than four months to live."

"You never know, Sydney. It could be a lot longer. There is no way a doctor can accurately predict how many months a person has to live with this type of cancer. You might luck out and live for a year or more."

"Or it could be less. I wouldn't want my life extended unless I'm one hundred percent functional. Once everything starts to go it will be time to call it quits," I said.

"Chair or couch today?" he asked.

"I think I'll sit," I answered and sat down facing him.

"By the way, doctor Miller. I'm pretty sure I'm being followed," I said.

He looked at me with a surprised expression on his face and said, "Not this again."

"This time I'm absolutely positive," I replied.

"Sydney, we've been through this before. You thought you were being followed by a black van, then you thought you were wrong and weren't being followed. Now, once again, you think you are being followed. You're being paranoid. You are not being followed. No one has any reason to follow you. You have to put this to rest."

"How did you know it was a black van? I don't remember telling you that," I asked.

"I'm sure you did. Now, what are we talking about today? What would you like to discuss?" he replied.

"I don't have a whole lot more to talk about. I tried to buy a gun this weekend. Didn't happen, though. For some reason the background check is holding things up. Strange, don't you think?"

"I don't know anything about how that works. So, should we get started here?" he replied.

I watched his nicely tanned face turn red due to what I could only determine was guilt. "Is there something you would like to tell me, Doctor?" I asked him.

"I don't know what you are talking about. Why would I want to tell you something? I have nothing to tell you," he replied.

"I just thought maybe there was. Anyway, I would like to tell you about Presley. Isn't that a wonderful name? Presley. I just love saying it."

"Just who is Presley?" he asked.

In 2007, I retired at the age of fifty-two. This wasn't a hard decision as I had put in thirty years with L&L

Consulting and was ready for a change. I had made good money, had plenty of savings, and had a fantastic retirement plan. Selling my apartment and leaving Chicago, however, was not an easy thing for me to do. I had lived there since I had graduated from college. In the end, though, I decided a nice quiet place away from the hustle and bustle would be good for me. And, so, I bought my home in the country outside of Munster.

All the houses in my neighborhood were built on large wooded lots, giving us the privacy we desired and had paid for. I could see my neighbors' houses in the winter but, during the summer, the trees shielded them. It was a perfect place to live and I loved it. That is, until my neighbors, the Finnegans, decided they needed another dog and brought Presley home from the shelter.

I liked most dogs. I never had a dog because my job took me away from home so much. I had thought about getting a dog after I retired, but I wanted to travel so I put it on the back burner.

I didn't like all dogs. I didn't like dogs that weren't well-trained. If a dog tried to jump on me, I automatically responded by kneeing him in his chest and knocking him over. I hated barking dogs and never understood why their owners taught them to speak. I especially didn't like dogs that barked day and night. Poor Presley was this type of dog. You really couldn't blame him, as it was the Finnegans' decision to keep him outside.

The Finnegans and I were friendly, as neighbors go. I finally decided after Presley's barking continued to keep me awake night after night, to talk to them. I took a walk over to their house and barely made it into the house before Presley tried to jump on me. It was obvious he was untrained and undisciplined.

We discussed my problem with Presley and they said he didn't like to be tied up. I suggested that they install an electric dog fence. That way he could have the freedom to roam the yard without being tied or straying into a neighbor's property. They said they would think about it and, after we visited a little longer, I left hoping that they would resolve the matter.

Nothing changed. The dog's barking continued to keep me awake and I got angrier and angrier. I started calling the Finnegans, waking them up, saying if I couldn't sleep then I was going to be damn sure they couldn't either. Words were exchanged and the war began.

"You killed a dog?" Dr. Miller said.

"You always get ahead of the story, don't you?" I answered. "Just hang in there. I'm getting there. Do you have a dog?"

"Actually, we have two dogs. Although they belong to all the family, River is mostly mine. He tolerates the rest of the family when I'm not home, but once I walk through that door, he only has time for me," Dr. Miller answered.

"What type of dogs are they?" I asked him.

"River is a Yorkie. He only weighs about six pounds. The other dog is a golden retriever. Maxie is her name. Beautiful dog, but she sheds a lot. She is great with the kids, though."

"Do you keep them both in the house?" I inquired.

"Of course. I would never subject a dog to living alone outside. That makes no sense," he replied.

"Exactly."

I finally decided that I was not going to win the war with the Finnegans by being nasty. Waking them in the middle of the night because Presley was keeping me awake was no answer to this problem. I called them, asked if I could stop by around six to talk, and they agreed.

I drove to a local pet store where I bought a chew toy and a bag of treats for Presley. Next, I went to Sammy's Florist Shop and bought a bouquet of flowers that I planned to take to the Finnegans, along with a nice bottle of wine that I had at home.

We visited for a while and discussed Presley's barking problem. They mentioned the fence and said that they had heard it hurt the dogs, so they had decided against it. I smiled and said I understood. After a little more conversation, I apologized for my late-night phone calls and asked them to forgive me. We all finally laughed about it and decided to let bygones be bygones and start fresh.

I told them that I would be away for a few weeks on vacation. I was going out west, mostly sightseeing, but I planned to spend a few days in Vegas. I asked if they would keep an eye on my place and they said they were more than happy to watch it for me.

I flew out of O'Hare the next morning for Vegas. After spending a few days gambling and seeing a few shows, I rented a car and headed south. I spent the next six days sightseeing. Then I was back in Vegas, on a plane, and headed home. I actually enjoyed the trip and slept like a baby thanks to no barking dogs to keep me awake.

"So, Presley was dead when you got home. Did anyone even figure you had poisoned the dog treats?" Dr. Miller said.

"Presley wasn't dead. It wasn't his fault the Finnegans made him stay tied up all the time. I'd bark my head off, too, if someone did that to me."

"The wine. You poisoned the wine, didn't you? You killed the Finnegans?"

"The dog was gone when I got home. That was the only thing that mattered. I had my peaceful home back."

"Why didn't you just kill the dog, for God's sake?" Dr. Miller practically yelled.

"The dog only did what dogs do. It wasn't his fault those people tied him up. Killing him wouldn't have made a difference. Those idiots would have just gone and gotten another dog to torment. They needed to be stopped and I needed my sleep."

"Good god, Sydney. Please tell me there aren't any more bodies."

"Those are the last ones, Doc. The Finnegans were the last people I poisoned."

"Thank God," he replied. "Thank God."

He was quiet for a few seconds, thinking about something. I watched his face change expressions as he realized something.

"When was that? When did the Finnegans die?" he asked.

"That was about nine months ago. It was right after that I found out I had brain cancer." I replied.

"Sydney, do you still have any of the poison left?" he asked.

"I think there are still five capsules left. I guess I should dump them somewhere. Maybe dig a hole and bury them. It's a little tricky. I don't know how to get rid of it. I don't want to put it down the sink or flush it. I haven't figured it out yet. I don't want to accidentally kill anyone else. Can you believe I made that stuff when I was twenty-eight years old and it still works? Never lost its potency.

Perhaps I should write down how I did this for future reference."

"Don't bother. It's all here in my notes," Dr. Miller replied.

"Where do we go from here? I guess we're done with our sessions. So, is this it?" I asked.

"How about we stay in touch as long as you're able? I'll be compiling all my notes and recordings throughout the next few weeks and I'm sure I'll have some questions for you. Perhaps we could still meet once or twice a week for a while. How does that sound to you?"

"Sounds fine. Set up the appointments and let me know. I'm pretty much available any time now. The only thing I seem to do anymore is see doctors."

"I'll have Jennie call you with the times."

"Bye, Doc."

Twenty-six

On Wednesday afternoon, I received a phone call from Steve, who worked at Jason's Sporting Goods. He informed me that my background check was fine and I could pick up the gun I wanted to purchase at my convenience. It seemed that the computers had been down with some type of glitch over the holiday weekend and that had caused the mix-up.

Perhaps Dr. Miller was right and I was just paranoid. I was sure the feds had stopped my purchase. If I was wrong about that maybe I was also wrong about being followed.

As soon as I hung up the phone, I drove to the sporting goods store to pick up the gun. I finished all the necessary paperwork, paid the fee for the conceal carry license, and took my brand-new Glock G43 home with me. I spent the rest of the afternoon practicing how to load and unload it.

On Thursday, I had an idea. I was still concerned about how to dispose of the rest of the Doll's Eye poison. There was no scenario that I could think of that was one hundred percent safe. If I dumped it down the sink, would it get into the water system? How diluted would it have to be before it was harmless? If I buried it and years from now someone planted a garden in that spot, or a dog buried a bone there, would it have leaked into the soil and still be potent? Why did I even care? I certainly didn't want my nephew and niece to find it when they cleaned out the house. I had to get rid of it before I died.

After searching the web, I decided to call 'Chicago's Number One--Rides for Fun', a helicopter touring service that you could hire to sightsee the Chicago area by air. I asked if they would allow me to drop my dog's ashes out of the helicopter into Lake Michigan and they said no problem. I booked a flight for the following day, hoping the weather would allow the bird to take off.

I drove to Jason's Sporting Goods and shopped for a small metal waterproof container. I was surprised at the large selection the store had on hand and I finally picked one that looked the right size to hold a dog's ashes plus a couple of bricks. I was about to have a burial at sea.

On the way home I was sure I saw the silver sedan following me. Enough. I knew this was not my imagination and I was sick of this little game they were playing.

On Thursday, I drove to Chicago the long way. I managed to lose the sedan somewhere around Des Plaines and a few hours later I was high in the sky over Lake Michigan. I was sorry I hadn't taken this ride before. The view was breathtaking and I loved it. I asked the pilot to take me out as far as possible so I could drop the ashes. He turned the helicopter away from Chicago and, as I looked back at the city, I watched the skyline grow smaller. Finally, he motioned this was it, so I handed him the box and he let it go. He circled the spot a few times and I watched as the box dropped into the lake and sank.

The final five capsules were buried at sea in a waterproof box. One less thing to worry about.

On Friday, Jennie called from Dr. Miller's office and asked if I could come in the following Tuesday. Dr. Miller had some stuff he wanted to go over with me.

Twenty-seven

I was preparing for bed when I heard the doorbell ring. It was late and it was rare for me to have company, so I was a little concerned about who could be calling. I wondered if I should get my gun but decided against it. I slipped on my robe and went to answer the door.

Before I opened the door, I glanced out the window and saw a silver sedan sitting in my driveway. My heart jumped. What in the world was happening? There was no way to avoid this. The lights were on in the house and they had probably seen me look out the window. As far as I could tell, I had no option but to answer the door.

"You are Sydney Geyer, is that correct?" one of the men asked me.

"I am. Can I help you with something?" I replied.

"We have a few questions to ask you. Would you mind if we come in?" the same man said.

"Why in the world would I let you into my home this time of night? I don't know you. Please, step back and leave before I call the police," I responded.

Both men reached into their pockets and pulled out wallets holding FBI identifications and badges.

I took my time looking at them and then asked them to come in and sit down.

"What can I do for you Agents Peterson and McRoy?"

Is there a problem?"

"Special Agent in Charge," they both said in unison.

"Sorry. Special Agents in Charge. Is there something I can do for you?" I asked.

"We are investigating the deaths of your former neighbors, the Finnegans. It has been brought to our attention that the police never interviewed you. We were wondering if there is any information you might have regarding their deaths," Agent Peterson said.

"I don't. I was out of town—out west on vacation when that happened. I only heard about it when I got back home."

"We believe they died the night before you left for vacation and that you were at their home that night. Is that correct?"

"I'm sorry. I seem to be confused. First, I don't understand why the FBI would be investigating their deaths and not the police. Second, I thought it was an accident. And third, I don't like your tone. Should I call my lawyer? Are you accusing me of something?" I replied.

Special Agent in Charge McRoy looked at me and said, "We would like permission to search your home."

"Now? You come barging in here at this time of night and tell me you want to search my home? I don't think so. Do you have a warrant? I'm asking you to leave, right now." I got up and started towards the front door.

"We have the warrant. We only asked to be polite. Sit

down, Sydney. It's going to be a long night," said Special Agent in Charge McRoy. "Where do you keep your gun?"

It was a long night. The two agents searched every possible hiding place in my home. When they found the safe hidden in my bedroom, I opened it for them. They were respectful of my belongings, which surprised me. In the movies, you always see everything thrown around and the rooms are left a mess.

Finally, having found nothing of interest to them, they said their farewells and left. I went into the bathroom and threw up.

Twenty-eight

It was Tuesday afternoon and I was sitting in Dr. Miller's office. I had just finished telling him about the FBI showing up at my home on Saturday night.

"Do you even have any idea how traumatic it was?" I asked him. "They show up right as I'm about to go to bed. With a warrant, no less, and search my entire house. It took hours. They didn't leave until after four in the morning. And, it seems to me that they knew just what they were looking for. You don't search the toes of every pair of sox unless you are looking for something small."

"They didn't find anything?" Dr. Miller asks me.

"No. They didn't. There was nothing to find."

"What about the poison? The capsules? They didn't find them?"

"They did not. Because, they no longer exist. I got rid of them. I guess my timing is pretty good. If I had held on to them a few days longer, I might have been caught."

"You got rid of them?"

"That's right. Let's just say they've been buried in a place where they will never be found."

"I see. Well, I have a couple of questions I'd like to ask you. There are some areas of your story that I'd like to fill in before I turn my report over to the FBI."

"About that, Doctor. I've changed my mind. I no

longer want you to say anything to them after I die. I don't see that anything good will come from it. Some of these deaths go back so far that they have been forgotten or there is no one left who needs closure or cares. It may be selfish, but I see no point in it now. I've told you my story. There's no need for anyone else to ever know."

"But, Sydney, that was the whole point in your coming to see me."

"At first. However, I realized as our sessions continued that it was really more for me. I needed to get it out and tell someone. Do you know how hard it is to go for years having to keep something like this to yourself? I thought, knowing that I was dying, that this was the best thing to do. Now I realize I just needed to talk. You've helped me immensely but it stops here."

"I'd like you to reconsider."

"No. What I've told you stays between you and me. Is that understood?" I asked.

"Well, that may be a little difficult," he said.

"And, why would that be? Because you've already told the FBI? You have, haven't you? That's why I've spent weeks being followed. That's why they invaded my home on Saturday. You fucking son of a bitch. You told them!"

"Now, Sydney, let me explain. You've got it all wrong."

"Do I? I knew it. At least, I suspected it. It was way too much of a coincidence that shortly after I start seeing you,

I'm being followed. I mention it to you and you tell them to back off a little. The black van. That's how you knew what color car was following me."

"Wait. You're blowing this all out of proportion. You know I can't divulge patient-doctor confidentiality."

"You didn't tell them what I had done, did you? You told them you thought I might be planning something illegal. That way you knew they would start watching me. You bastard. You told them about the poison, didn't you? That's why they knew exactly what they were looking for. I thought you might be involved in them watching me. I just didn't know how far you went."

"I didn't say anything. I promise. You're just being paranoid again. You've got to settle down so we can discuss this calmly."

"Calmly? You expect me to —"

"Sydney, are you okay? Let me get you some water."

I heard his voice but it seemed like it was coming from a distant place. I looked up and saw him standing over the top of me.

"Here, let me help you up."

He helped me into a chair and handed me a glass of water.

"How long have you been having seizures?"

"For a while now. This is the worst one yet. This damn disease is going to kill me one way or the other," I said.

"You want to lie down for a while?" he asked.

"I'm fine. I just want to go home," I said.

"I don't think it's safe for you to drive."

"Probably not, but I'm doing it anyway." And, with that, I got up and left his office.

Twenty-nine

I don't remember the drive home. I do remember being so pissed off I couldn't see straight. Dr. Miller had gone too far.

I walked into my home and headed straight for the bed. I was exhausted. That seizure was definitely the worst one and it had taken a lot out of me. I decided to call Dr. Fuller in the morning. Perhaps there was something she could give me to help control them.

Dr. Fuller was upset with me. I had called her and she wanted to see me immediately. So, here I was sitting in her office being chewed out.

"Why didn't you call me the minute you had the first seizure? You're walking around with a brain tumor and you don't think it's important enough to call me when you have a seizure? All right. Let's draw some blood. I need to do that anyway, so might as well do it while you are here. I'm going to write you a prescription for an AED. It should help with your seizures. I want you to take it as prescribed—don't miss a dosage. You are not to drive. Is that clear?"

"But I can't just not drive," I said.

"You either stop driving or I will revoke your license. Let's give this medication a week or so to work. If you are free of seizures for two weeks, I'll reconsider the driving part. I want you to check in with me every day or so and let me know how you are doing. You understand what I'm saying, Sydney?"

"Yes, I understand. I'm not stupid. At least, not yet," I replied.

After leaving her office, I drove to the pharmacy, picked up my prescription, and drove home. I decided that I would stick around the house for the next few days and monitor the medication. And, rest. I seemed to be getting more tired each day.

Thirty

I stuck to my guns and stayed home for the next few days. I checked in with Dr. Fuller, as promised, and she said it seemed like the medication was doing its job.

I read, watched TV, did some yard work, and fumed. The more I thought about Dr. Miller, the madder I got. That bastard had betrayed me. I went to him with the assurance that nothing I said would be repeated and he had gone to the FBI.

I thought about the satisfaction I felt after killing Herb and Pat and Tony and the rest of them. Except for Charles. I never got that feeling after killing him. He had hurt me physically and even though I killed him, he didn't suffer. The Doll's Eye poison was so fast-acting that he barely felt a thing.

Now it was Dr. Miller's turn to die. My poison might be at the bottom of Lake Michigan but I still had my gun.

Thirty-one

I was up and out of bed early Monday morning. The anticipation of what I was about to do was so great I was almost trembling. I was going to be Dr. Miller's first patient of the day and he didn't even know it. Today he would get his comeuppance for betraying me.

Dr. Fuller had said I was doing pretty well, but I knew better. I was sleeping more, and I had some memory loss. There were times I couldn't remember what I had just done or said. That, along with the seizures, was a clear indication to me that it was all uphill from here. It was only a matter of time before I started losing body functions and the ability to move around.

If I was going to punish Dr. Miller, it had to be done while I was still physically able to get around. No time like the present, as the saying goes.

I arrived at his office a few minutes before nine. Jennie wasn't in yet so I walked right into his office and shut the door. Dr. Miller was sitting behind his desk, studying some papers. He glanced up and looked surprised to see me.

"Sydney, I don't remember you having an appointment this morning?" he inquired.

"I don't. I just thought I would come in and clear the air. I'll only be here a minute or two. This will be the last time I see you. I think we should discuss a few things that are still bothering me."

"If that's the case, I'm glad you came in. I never want to finish up with a patient and leave loose ends. How can I help you this morning? Fortunately, I don't have any patients today and I can give you a little time."

He stayed behind his desk. I reached over and pulled up a chair. I sat down, facing him.

"I have to say, Doctor, that I'm disappointed in you. I put a lot of trust in you and you betrayed me. I haven't slept well in days now and you know my rest is important to me. I'm sorry it has to end this way, but I don't see any alternative."

"What do you mean? End this way. Sydney, you have this all wrong. I only did what I thought was necessary to keep you doing something stupid."

"So now you admit that you had the FBI following me?" I asked.

"I've had enough of this. I'd like you to leave my office. I have work to do and nothing I say to you will ever convince you that you are wrong. You need to leave right now," Dr. Miller replies and starts to stand up.

"Sit down, Doctor. I'll leave when I'm ready. We're not done talking." I open my purse, take out my new gun, and point it at him.

"Sydney, what, what are you doing? Put that away."

"Did I tell you I bought a gun? Pretty, isn't it?" I said.

"Funny thing is that I never in my life thought a gun would be my weapon of choice. Probably wouldn't be now if I hadn't disposed of my poison. I haven't even fired it yet. I don't think I could possibly miss when I'm this close to my target. What about you? Do you think I could miss?"

"Sydney, please. Put that away. Let's talk this out."

"Tell me the truth. Did you sic the feds on me? Yes or no. Just tell me the truth."

"Kind of. All right, yes. They were already following you and then they talked to me and I might have said something. I'm sorry, but I was afraid you would do something foolish. I had to protect...

"Who? Who were you protecting?"

"I don't know. Whoever. Myself. You scare me and I was afraid. I figured if you were being watched I would be safe."

"Well, where are they now? Where are your protectors that will keep you safe from me now?" I yelled.

"If you kill me, you will spend the rest of what life you have left in jail. Is that what you want? You won't get the care you are going to need in a prison hospital. Think about what you are doing. Just leave now and I'll forget this ever happened."

As he talked, his arm brushed against some papers and they fell to the floor next to his desk. He bent down to pick them up, casually opened a desk drawer as he sat back up, reached in, and pulled out a gun. Before I had time to react, he pointed it at me and pulled the trigger.

His first shot hit me in the right shoulder making me drop my gun. "What the fuck? Why did you do that?" I glanced down at my gun lying on the floor.

"Dealing with nuts like you always puts me at risk. Don't look so shocked, Sydney. Did you really think you were invincible? Someone should have put you down years ago. You are, without a doubt, the most cold-blooded, heartless bitch I have ever met."

His second shot killed me.

Epilogue

He was sitting in his waiting room thinking about what had just happened. He had not only murdered Sydney, but he had also contaminated the crime scene. He had used Sydney's gun to shoot a hole in his office wall and then made sure none of his fingerprints were on the gun. Hopefully, he had done enough to cover his ass.

This was the first time he had killed anything. He wasn't a hunter and had never experienced the thrill of taking down a buck or watching a duck fall from the sky after being shot. He was not a violent man yet he couldn't shake the feeling that came over him as he watched Sydney die. He enjoyed it. Now he understood what Sydney meant when she said killing gave her satisfaction and made her feel powerful. He had felt those emotions as he watched her die. He had been excited almost to the point of arousal. He liked the way it made him feel and at the same time, it sickened him.

His office was now considered a crime scene and had been taken over by the police. They were waiting for the coroner to arrive. The police had informed him that CSI had also been notified and would be there shortly. No one was allowed back into the doctor's office.

Ten minutes after the police arrived on the scene the FBI walked in and tried to take over. FBI Special Agent in Charge James Carroll explained to the police detective, Bill

O'Reilly, that they had been watching Sydney Geyer for the past six weeks and this was their case. Detective O'Reilly then informed the Agent that a murder had taken place in his jurisdiction and they would be handling it. There was no need for the FBI's involvement.

Finally, after a few more minutes of arguing over whom the case belonged to, the police detective told the FBI agent that he would be willing to share his findings with him. That being settled the FBI agent directed his attention to Dr. Miller.

"Doctor, can you give me a statement as to what happened here? Of course, we will need you to come to our office later for a detailed explanation. Right now, could you just give us your version of what happened here? Do you want an attorney present?"

"I see no reason for an attorney. Sydney didn't have an appointment this morning. She just walked in, sat down, and started to talk. She wanted to say goodbye, she said. The more she talked the angrier she got. She thought I had told you about all the people she had killed. It didn't make any difference what I said, she didn't believe me. Then she pulled a gun out of her purse and pointed it at me. I managed to get my gun out of my desk and I shot her. I didn't want to kill her. I hit her in her arm. I thought that would stop her but she fired at me anyway. Thank God, she missed. I had no choice but to shoot again and that shot killed her."

"She fired at you after being hit in the arm?"

"Yes," the doctor replied. "I lucked out. I can't believe that her shot missed me and hit the wall."

"There will be an investigation into this, Doctor, but I don't think there is any question that it was self-defense," Special Agent in Charge Carroll said. "We're sorry that it ended this way, as we had some questions we would have liked to have asked her."

"I think I'll be able to help you there," Dr. Miller replied. "I have the recordings of our sessions which I'll give you. She killed eighteen people and never had any regrets over any of them. Sydney was a psychopath personified. No one would ever have been able to help her. She wanted to kill me because in her mind I betrayed her. She knew your men were following her and she decided it could only be because of me."

Special Agent in Charge Carroll didn't say anything for a few seconds. "Eighteen? She killed eighteen people? We had no idea it was that many," he finally said.

"Young, old, and in between. It made no difference to her. If you crossed Sydney, you were dead. I think you will have the answers to some unsolved cases when you listen to these tapes. There are people she killed and no one even suspected it was murder."

"By the way," Dr. Miller continued, "what made you start following her to begin with?"

"When she left our office in Chicago a little over six weeks ago, we decided to follow up. It was easy to find out who she was. Cameras all over the building, you know. Not knowing her story, we decided to keep an eye on her and see if it would lead anywhere. Then, of course, we found out she was seeing you."

"You knew when you questioned me that I couldn't tell you anything about Sydney. I take doctor-patient confidentiality very seriously," said Dr. Miller.

"Yes, and even though you didn't tell us in so many words that you were concerned for your safety, it was obvious that you were worried."

"As I said," Dr. Miller replied, "she thought I had given you information about our sessions. She was becoming more hostile toward me. When she mentioned she was thinking about buying a gun, I decided it was time to make sure mine was loaded and handy. I can't believe she thought I would turn her in."

"But you did tell us about the Finnegans, Doctor. Did you know that we were ready to stop our surveillance of her? If you hadn't given us that little piece of information we probably would have just stopped and moved on."

"When you talked to me a little over a week ago, she had just told me about the Finnegans. It had been fourteen years between her killings. When I found out that she had just recently murdered the Finnegans, I didn't know if she would stop. That's why I mentioned that you might want to look into their last visitor.

"And, look for pills. Remember, doctor, you mentioned pills."

Dr. Miller sighed. "A couple of days sooner and you would have found them. Sydney had a knack for being a step ahead of everything."

"Where are they? Do you know?"

"All she told me is that they are buried somewhere."

"Well," replied the agent, "You did what you had to do. It's a shame it ended this way."

"I suppose I should be sorry I said anything. I suppose in some sense I did betray her, but what in God's name was I supposed to do? She was a monster and I was hoping you would find the poison and have some evidence to arrest her on. Anything to get her off the streets and behind bars. You know Sydney only had a few months to live. When she first came to see me, she intended that I turn the tapes over to the FBI after she died. She changed her mind later on, but I still intended to turn them over to you. I think you will be very shocked at what you find out when you listen to those tapes," Dr. Miller said.

"I don't know, doctor. I think we've pretty much heard and seen it all," Special Agent in Charge Carroll said.

"Yes, I suppose you have. I just think that a woman serial killer is more shocking. I wonder if you ever met anyone like Sydney. I certainly never had, until now. The world is better off without her."

"Well, from what you've told me, you had no choice but to kill her."

"You're right. I had no choice."

About the Author

I'm retired and live a quiet life in Indiana. I have three sons and two grandsons. I also have a few step-grandkids. I'm never sure how many as that number changes from time to time. I'm still waiting for that great-grandchild to show up so I have someone my age to play with.

I enjoy a good laugh and love dumb jokes. Reading has always been my passion and I read a couple of books a week. I've also designed some websites and maintain them in my spare time.

I was born in Idaho seventy-six years ago. Who would have thought that someday I'd be publishing a book? It's a dream come true.

For most of my life, I've written short stories and poems for amusement. I never really took my writing seriously until recently. Not too long ago I wrote *Blueberries and Bears and My Brother's Shoes*, a book about growing up in the forties and fifties. After self-publishing it and giving it to friends and family to read, they encouraged me to start getting serious about my writing.

We moved a lot while I was growing up, finally settling in a small town in Wisconsin when I was in the fifth grade. We lived a few houses away from a little park where we used to play ball, which gave me the idea for the first chapter of Crossing Sydney. That's also where the reality ends and the fiction (that suddenly grew into my first published book available to the public) begins.

I'm hoping that the ideas will continue to flow and that I'll be writing for a long time to come.

www.susanlpare.com